SUSPENDING REALITY

INTERIORS BY

BENJAMIN NORIEGA ORTIZ

WRITTEN WITH
LINDA O'KEEFFE

THE MONACELLI PRESS

CONTENTS

INTRODUCTION

When I was a child in Puerto Rico we moved often, but my mother took a lot of care in customizing each new home. She sewed elaborate lambrequins and valances for each window and embroidered my bedspread with a large, cursive monogram. Because of her, I came to see interior decoration as a life-enhancing endeavor. While she was rearranging our rooms with her fascination of the moment—neo-Spanish furniture, Danish modern furniture, wallpaper—I would map out each room's dimensions and rectify all their architectural imperfections on graph paper. It may have been my way of coping with impermanence.

The house we lived in during my teenage years was contemporary and starkly white. By that time, I'd become my mother's willing accomplice. I never stopped experimenting with décor. It was as if I were auditioning for some TV makeover show! Or, more accurately, I gave the opinions and she gave the instructions. When I was thirteen we cofurnished the family's weekend apartment on Luquillo Beach. In the living room we paired rattan chairs and gold-flecked carpets with cork baseboards and I painted a huge, Marimekko-like mural on the dining room wall.

While attending the School of Architecture at the University of Puerto Rico, I discovered music, dance, and photography. I made ceramic sculptures with Jaime Suarez, who is now viewed as one of Latin America's most influential contemporary artists. I knew Jorge Rigau way before he became a Fellow of the AIA. I was instinctively drawn to people who somehow connected me to a larger world I hadn't yet encountered.

Around that time I also fell in love with all things Italian and learned to speak the language fluently in preparation for a post-graduation summer in Europe. It was a revelation to stand in the Uffizi Gallery in Florence, close enough to touch paintings by Titian and Botticelli. Caravaggio is still one of my greatest inspirations, and I literally cried when I first saw the compositional chiaroscuro in his *John the Baptist*. I tooled around Rome on a moped, and I still have a stack of the proportion sketches I made of Bernini's colonnade in Saint Peter's Square. I was in Venice when Peggy Guggenheim's modern art collection was inaugurated into a museum and from my bunk in a hostel I dreamed of checking into The Bauers, which is now one of my favorite hotels.

When I walked across a rickety, makeshift bridge of gondolas to attend mass during the Festa del Redentore on the one day each year when Palladio's sixteenth-century church and its central axis is accessible from across the Giudecca Canal, I was in heaven. As fate would have it I got ill in Paris and briefly stayed in the Hotel-Dieu hospital on the left bank next to Notre-Dame so I had the opportunity to study the cathedral's fourteenth-century facade from a front-row bed. When I recovered I traded Gothic for the radical modernism of the Centre Pompidou, which was still highly controversial for the revolution it caused by turning the worlds of architecture and art upside down.

I moved to Manhattan—my second adult trip away from Puerto Rico and my first time living alone—to attend Columbia University and pursue an additional master's degree in architecture and urban design. Then as now, I preferred to collect experiences to objects, so I was always anticipating my next trip, but I found that stepping out into the city could also be just as enriching as traveling. I now call it my hometown.

After graduation I worked for a small architectural firm. While I was supervising a townhouse renovation in Chelsea for Dina Merrill's son I heard about a vacancy in John Saladino's office. I dropped off my résumé the next day and assumed the chance of me working alongside one of the country's most celebrated designers was slim. Nevertheless I put my insecurities aside, set up an interview, and was hired on the spot to assist the head designer in the firm's architectural department.

For my first assignment, the refurbishment of a plastic surgeon's office, I assembled a 200-plus-page folder of specific finishes so John could supervise how walls abutted baseboards and how hinges attached to doors. His attention to the smallest details of every phase of the project was astounding. His designs routinely incorporated historical precedents, so he kept an extensive library. It gave me instant access to illustrations of every type of column, balustrade, portico, or fresco. Plus, I was the one person in the office who understood all the perfectly pronounced Italian phrases that rolled off his tongue. I was only in my mid-twenties, but I must have come across as an older soul. Within two years, John made me his head designer. It's impossible to quantify how much I learned from everyone at Saladino's firm, where I stayed seven more years. I worked alongside Brian Boyle, the firm's head architect, on many projects. Apart from being educational, it was enriching to execute John's exquisitely tasteful, graceful aesthetic. His work is serious and spectacular. I became almost nonchalant about museum-quality art and furniture because I dealt with it so routinely.

As my personal style developed, I found myself drawn to sculptural, arty, whimsical, edgy, and attainable interiors. By 1992 I'd built up the confidence to make a break and open my own firm. As if being out on my own wasn't eventful enough, I soon designed my first ground-up project in Amagansett, with my former partner Rene Fuentes-Chao. It was for a compact beach house, which I re-thought from the inside out. It lacked any kind of regular fenestration, but the open-plan interior, which I'd set on a central axis and designed with an enfilade, was completely cohesive. Thanks to bleached-pine floors, sea-foam green upholstery, and a mosquito-net draped platform bed, it had charm and attitude in equal proportions. My favorite detail was an outdoor shower under the shade of a weathered oak tree—one wall was mirrored to reflect a tapered row of boxwoods. Fortunately *Elle Décor* featured the project as a cover story; the string of ensuing international press coverage introduced me to new clients.

At its core, my work today adheres to the same classical sense of organization that holds together most traditional projects, but I don't follow any prescribed rules of symmetry. I prefer a choreography of opposites—rustic with highly polished, straight legs with cabrioles, a camel-back sofa with a more angular counterpart, nineteenth-century pieces juxtaposed with contemporary, wood with metal, laser-cut with handmade. I like to challenge the acceptable notions of "good taste" by throwing something ironic or unexpected into every project, even the most serious, dark paneled library.

Each person relates to color differently; they say people either have auditory or visual memories, but I think I have a color-based memory. I am hopeless at remembering the name of clients' children, but I can recall the exact green we used in a kitchen fifteen years ago. An affinity for color helps me incorporate important art in client projects as well. Hanging art centrally or symmetrically feels predictable to me. So does configuring furniture around a room's chief feature, like a large sculpture, a set of French doors, or a mantel. I don't understand the impulse to plan an entire scenario around a fireplace, a wall-mounted television, a piano, or anything else that's only animated during the short amount of time it's actually in use. I'd rather create a focal point out of something less expected. I also don't believe in keeping precious objects tucked away behind glass. My mother kept our best china

locked up, but I thought it was beautiful and should be appreciated every day, so once when no one was around I mounted it all to the dining-room wall.

I've thankfully reached a point in my career where I don't need to take on projects for budgetary considerations alone. I'm inclined to walk away from a commission if I don't perceive any possibility for adventure or a challenge. Some of my favorite and most frequently published projects, in fact, are small in scale or were produced on a shoestring. I thrive on having to be flexible—I've also seen how a surfeit of money can negatively impact a project. As Albert Hadley used to say, it puts no limit on the number of ugly things people can acquire!

Clients who come to me seem to share my appreciation for negative space, which is just as well because it plays a large role in my work. Japanese architect Tadao Ando and Antwerp-based designer Alex Vervoordt—who I think of as spatial masters—both refer to it as the "fullness of emptiness." They achieve exuberance via restraint, and their use of materiality celebrates the process of aging or *wabi sabi*, so their work always appears universal and timeless. I design rooms to stand the test of time so eventual scuffed surfaces, faded or frayed textiles, and small paint chips don't ruin the entire look. Whenever clients put "pristine condition" or "brand new" at the top of their list of priorities, I gently remind them of Salvador Dalí's suggestion not to live in fear of perfection because you can never reach it! Or whenever a client holds out for the "ultimate chair" or covets something primarily because it'll likely impress a colleague, I suggest we circle back and make choices that resonate on a meaningful level. I'm inspired and motivated by trends as much as the next designer, but it doesn't feel paradoxical to ignore them, either. Nothing is passé if it enhances the present.

It's hard for me to decipher whether the hotels I design influence my residential work or vice versa. Either way, the two overlap and inform each other. Apart from scale, I think the same principles can apply to the design of a pocketbook or a building. In all cases detailing, convenience, human proportion, beauty, and a transformative experience are crucial. There's one technical distinction—I still sketch my residential interiors, while I use 3-D CAD technology to plan my hotels. I wouldn't dream of showing a computer-generated layout of a house or apartment to a client; they're too perfectly resolved and impersonal. (Also, the one time I tried that I lost the commission!) I prefer the spontaneity of hand drawings—it's easy to change something midway through a meeting or at any stage of planning.

I'm heavily invested in everything I create, but I never take my aesthetic or myself too seriously. Thankfully I'm never thought of as the go-to person for authentic period restorations, and if ever the prospect arises I suggest using a curator rather than a designer. My clients tend to be passionate about art or they're often in the fields of writing, music, fashion design, or photography. Bill Moyers defines creativity as "piercing the mundane to find the marvelous," and that type of innovation can happen if I'm lucky enough to collaborate with someone who opts to take the design road less travelled.

There's nothing worse than pretention, so I gravitate to clients who are somewhat easy-going as well. I interpret a lot from the way a client treats waiters when we first meet, and I read a lot into the way he or she dresses. Saladino expected his male staff to wear a suit and tie every day, but as soon as I launched my own firm I ditched my pinstripes. Apart from having one less choice to make each morning, my "uniform" of a black T-shirt and jeans doesn't distract from or compete with the flair in my work. It never serves as a topic of conversation, and it never upstages any fabric or color I propose! But more important, by dressing informally all the time, I show clients that I'm comfortable in my own skin. They immediately pick up on that and it encourages them to relax and be themselves as well; to not be on guard, uptight, or self-conscious. I can't think of a better way to begin a partnership.

CHAPTER 1

MAKING AN ENTRANCE

A sense of procession is important to all my projects. Normally I begin the approach to a large or prominent public area with a smaller scaled entryway or hall so that when you reach the main room you've registered the spatial progression. Perhaps you paused mid-stride, you looked around, you generally took it in. This is a tried-and-true technique for organizing space in a way that makes people appreciate it. I hardly invented it, but I swear by it.

That's not to say that I'm bullheaded when working alongside someone with a different or clear vision, even if it strikes me as counterintuitive at first. With certain clients, it's best to step into a facilitator role and just execute their desires in the most successful way possible. For example, I recently had an interesting discussion about spatial hierarchy with Ivanka and Donald Trump at a lush Miami golf club he owns. In my layout for the presidential suites there, I had proposed assigning the majority of space to the communal areas and bedrooms. Trump looked at my sketch, then immediately offered up another idea. Based on the old adage "you never get a second chance to make a first impression," he asked me to increase the square footage of the foyers—to the point where their size upstaged each of the other rooms in the suite. He wanted the guests to have an experience that made them feel regal from the moment they opened the door. He also reasoned, rightly, that they would be spending most of their time on the fairway or in the clubhouse, so smaller living and dining areas wouldn't leave them feeling deprived. Also, each suite features a wall of windows that showcases a panoramic view of the facility's manicured greens, and Trump envisioned a spacious entrance as a warm-up act to experiencing that spectacle. It was a high-drama strategy as well as a fascinating illustration of perception enhancing reality. I never stop learning from clients.

Without veering too far into Hallmark territory, I feel it is important to say that I do believe every ending signals a new beginning and a departure precedes every arrival. Don't many of your memories involve a situation where you were arriving or leaving? And can't you see the space where that memory was made clearly in your mind, still? I never underestimate the importance of simply crossing a threshold and I want every doorway in my projects to trigger a favorable reaction. I want whatever's on the other side to immediately invite, comfort, entertain, intrigue, calm, inspire, amuse, or nurture. If ever I have a delayed reaction when I step into a room—and even three seconds is too long—I know the décor is unresolved. Maybe the colors clash or a painting is askew. There's no stylistic harmony. No anchor for the furniture. Perhaps the lighting's too dim? Or maybe the high, angular back of a sofa feels confrontational and off-putting?

Another factor I keep in mind as I think about composition is this: an arrow might fly directly from point A to point B, but people rarely walk in a straight line. By nature, we meander. The eye similarly likes to wander, and it prefers being enticed rather than catapulted from one side of the room to the other. Luis Barragán called his process of gradually luring people through layers of space "architectural striptease," and that is a playful but effective description of what all designers try to accomplish. Making a successful room involves introducing focal points at intervals throughout—a piece of art, a jolt of color, curated displays of collections—to bait and delay us. It makes us savor our route. Sequencing helps each design element relate to its larger context, and choreography makes all the elements compatible and smooths transitions. Both of these involve retaining a macro mindset so be sure to adopt an overall awareness to build energy and flow within and between rooms.

In movies, staircases—another type of entryway—metaphorically signify journeys or psychological shifts. In real life, they're workaday traffic circulators. Like any object in a room, though, they still have enormous dramatic and sculptural potential. Whether it's showy or concealed, the proportion of any staircase needs to synch with human anatomy, and for this reason I often reference the golden mean and the Fibonacci numbers in my work. The architect Le Corbusier saw these mathematical ratios as the rhythmic roots of organic activity, "apparent to the eye and clear in their relations with one another." In other words, if a staircase's stringers, risers, and treads are disproportionate our subconscious perceives a stairway as an obstacle course.

Speaking of steps, I also advocate that people go barefoot in their homes whenever possible. Apart from giving yourself a spontaneous reflexology session, it has the hygienic benefit of not tracking in outdoor grime. Most important, going shoeless creates intimacy and informality and it demarcates the transition between public and private domains. In the country, we take mudrooms for granted. And even though the custom of removing shoes before entering someone's home is normal in many parts of the world, it still strikes many American city dwellers as novel or exotic. Not all of my clients adhere to my "no footwear" suggestion, but whenever they do it always has positive results. And by nodding to the ancient tradition that many devotees follow of shedding a worldly outer layer before entering a temple or shrine, it humbly proposes that we view our home as a true sanctuary—as we should.

LEFT An ethereal Upper East Side Manhattan foyer functions as a visual transition between a building's traditional hallways and an apartment's contemporary interior. An illuminated plinth bounces light onto a marble-tiled floor and elevates an antique terra-cotta horse. A bank of triple-pleated, silk organza veils an ebony grand piano in the living room beyond. PREVIOUS PAGES A 17-foot-tall, ivy-trellised tunnel leads to the main lobby of the Mondrian Soho Hotel in New York, which is set back 100 feet from the curb—it welcomes each guest like a horticultural red carpet.

LEFT A Long Island weekend house's otherwise-traditional entry is given a dose of drama with carpeted steps, double-height outdoor draperies, and tall steel topiary stands. The sense of grandeur established on the exterior stays with guests and influences how they view the interiors. ABOVE The house is nestled into the woods, so blue exterior facades bring the some of the sky to earth and, in the living room, a matte blue paint treatment inspired by Yves Klein's use of pigment covers a formerly exposed brick wall as well as helps to obscure the fireplace's off-central placement.

ABOVE Chairs with widely different provenances form a seating arrangement of all-white perches on a second-floor landing in Lenny Kravitz's Miami house. Their location at eye level with an oversized Moroccan chandelier that hangs in the adjacent staircase allows visitors to appreciate its intricate detailing. RIGHT The first floor of the same house features several variations of white—in a pearlized ocular artwork, upholstered onto a cabriole-legged chair, and in patent leather flooring—that transform what was a simple, scalloped archway into an ethereal portal.

LEFT Curtains constructed from Gretchen Bellinger's iconic Limousine Cloth dramatize the threshold of a handsome living room in a 10,000-square-foot Yorktown house. They also soften, diminish, and occasionally close off a view into a prominent paneled-wood staircase. Contemporary pieces, such as the set of Mario Bellini Cab chairs, add complexity to a collection otherwise comprised mainly of English and Chinese antiques. RIGHT Strategically placed furniture, art, and artifacts spill over into hallways and landings to create continuity in the transitions between rooms with different functions. Objects here are given prominence solely according to shape, size, texture, and color—not because of provenance or monetary value.

LEFT In the lobby of 30 Crosby Street, a downtown Manhattan loft building, a limited color palette and intriguingly sensual materials—a monolithic piece of alabaster, a leather-lined wall, thin latex curtains, a thickly carpeted floor, and a customized air fragrance—prompt residents to shed the stress caused by the commotion on the street and exhale deeply when they come home. ABOVE Iron casement doors and vaulted ceilings in Enoteca, the building's communal wine-tasting room, reference traditional cellars. A set of clear, acrylic chairs and a rug with a subtly orthogonal pattern harken back to the lobby's modern vibe and bring the room firmly into the present. OVERLEAF, LEFT A set of steel stairs cantilevering from a central wall connects the basement, where the entry to this apartment is located, to the living room on the ground floor. The first thing a guest encounters is an environment where every discernible surface is glazed in gold plate. OVERLEAF, RIGHT In a hallway leading to an apartment's backyard, a bank of curtains in a light Gretchen Bellinger wool lead the eye to a yellow sofa below a reinterpretation of Caravaggio's *Bacchino Malato*, a piece originally conceived for a *New York Magazine* editorial.

LEFT In a Hamptons weekend house, architect Brian E. Boyle designed a glass balcony to mediate the difference between ceiling heights that jump from 9 to 18 feet between the first and second floor, where guest bedrooms are located. ABOVE In a powder room, a frosted-glass door takes up fully a third of the glass wall that divides a boudoir-like sitting area from the rest of the space. It features a unique clear acrylic handle, opens on butterfly hinges, and its 9-foot-high metal frame is painted in Benjamin Moore's Navajo White to match the surrounding walls. OVERLEAF, LEFT Thanks to an oversized, rectangular mirror, a flowering ficus tree immediately outside the entry to a Palm Beach house becomes interior artwork. Maya Romanoff wallpaper initiates the mustard-colored textile theme, and a lamp sits off-center on a skirted table so as not to obscure the view. OVERLEAF, RIGHT In a Park Avenue apartment, a feather lampshade by ABYU Lighting plays off an elliptical archway and a traditional staircase with spindle rails and a lathed balustrade. A double-skirted tablecloth introduces a fashionable dimension in a project that revolved around the reuse of a client's large inventory of traditional furnishings.

OPEN-AIR THEATER

I wish I could live in the outdoor "room" I played in as a child at the beach, because in lots of ways its stark simplicity was ideal. All I needed for an entire summer of entertainment was a pair of shorts, flip-flops, suntan lotion, and a towel. I turned the towel into a makeshift wall for the hideaway we created from a fallen palm tree trunk, fanned-out fronds provided a ceiling, and raked sand served as a floor.

Outdoor living space is always considered a luxury, whether it's an apartment balcony or a huge tract of rural acreage. Whether yours is a canopied porch, a rooftop, a deck, a terraced garden, or a veranda, its design needs to resolve issues of privacy and shelter before it's able to provide comfort and relaxation. In an urban setting, a wall or fence usually provides a spatial boundary. In a broader landscape beds of flowers, pathways, boxwood hedges, or a pergola may provide visual organization. In all cases, a well-conceived design begins by addressing issues of over-exposure to neighbors, harsh wind, or glaring sun. This is where strategically placed umbrellas or high-backed chairs work wonders. Furniture placement is a forgone conclusion—it should always celebrate the view.

It's disconcerting when indoor and outdoor furniture match exactly, as if a cleaning crew momentarily placed everything outside while they spruced up the interior! Conversely, a complete stylistic departure—a Victorian tea folly or a tiki hut adjacent to a contemporary house—is even more jarring. Aim to keep things stylistically in sync so the end result feels simple, harmonious and sculptural.

The size of a designated area and its function—cooking, dining, sitting, swimming, conversing—determines the number of seats needed and the length of any table surfaces. As with my interiors, I prefer fewer, broader gestures so can I keep the number of elements in my "room" scenarios to a minimum. Close up as well as from a distance, overblown or busy arrangements read as clutter. Rather than a chaise, consider a frameless bed, round or square; it instills structure and anchors an area well. Plan for furniture to stay put once it's placed. Paradoxically, I also love hanging chairs, hammocks, rockers, porch swings, and any type of seating that moves. Motion epitomizes freedom and fun.

For color schemes, take direction from the immediate environment. I wouldn't dream of trying to upstage nature. I tend towards natural wood colors and easy-care upholstery or curtain fabrics in organic, muddier colors. I keep lighting minimal so that it glows at ground level and never points upward, where it might diminish the impact of the night sky.

CHAPTER 2

OPENING ACTS

The prospect of decorating a raw space can be daunting. It throws many people into a complete panic. I'm often asked, "Where do you begin? Do you search for the perfect carpet or sofa first? Do you draw inspiration from a piece of art? Do you map out a color scheme?" All of these questions have the same answer: yes and no. Despite what we see on those makeover TV shows, interior design isn't formulaic, it's not instantaneous, and you can't create a room armed only with a hot glue gun. Creating an interior is a process. To get off to a good start, acknowledge the uniqueness of every scenario.

A blank stage is similar to an empty room. Set designers, like interior designers, rely on tools such as form, balance, juxtaposition, proportion, rhythm, scale, color, texture, harmony, perspective, and spatial layering to create a mood. Take a moment and think about how many different operas, ballets, and plays you've seen—and how different each production was. Now think about the fact that set designers are able to conjure individual, memorable backdrops for such varied dramas on stages of roughly all the same size and shape. Creating a memorable interior takes a little bit of stagecraft, too—it's all about manipulating a finite space.

While a set designer's creativity only needs to hold your attention for a few hours, an interior designer's needs to address functional challenges that will help you live in a space happily for years. A loft, country house, or weekend cabin may look fabulous in a magazine, but you have no way of knowing if its main asset is simply being photogenic. Your home must set the stage for the characters in your life, otherwise it will be uncomfortable. Architect Buckminster Fuller was talking about arriving at a similar conclusion when he said: "I never think about beauty. I think only of how to solve the problem. But when I am finished, if the solution is not beautiful, I know it is wrong."

A room's basic structure—its square footage, ceiling height, window and door placement—determines its potential. But whether it has five windows or two, whether it has a vaulted or coffered ceiling is immaterial. If you have a space you must work with, there's no sense trying to judge it as better or worse than an idealized space you've seen somewhere else. No room has perfect credentials, so don't disparage idiosyncrasies and shortcomings. Treat them as incentives to become more inventive and original.

If necessary, begin by making a physical list of all your room's raw features. Try to stay impartial—think of yourself as a makeup artist whose job it is to coax the beauty out of the face of every actor appearing in a play. Once you have a clear idea of a room's function, assign it a disposition. My favorite dining rooms are gregarious and extroverted. I like kitchens to be open and friendly—convivial. Bedrooms should literally make you want to retire. Each of your rooms should also feel compatible with your personality. Think twice before you appropriate someone else's style, even if you admire it very much. One thing's for sure: agitated atmospheres are never ideal. As Luis Barragán put it, "Any architecture which does not express serenity is a mistake." Incorporate a core sense of calm into every room even, if it's bubbly and operatic overall.

I have a pretty classical sensibility, so my ideal project always includes an enfilade—a suite of rooms with doorways from one to the next aligned along a single axis. Architects devised this format in seventeenth-century France as an efficient way to usher people through staterooms in an orderly fashion. Enfilades are a formal and grand example of how to direct flow, but they make my point: every furnished room, no matter its size, needs a logical circulation path. If it doesn't have one, a room appears to be static and unsociable. We may not register it consciously, but our instinct makes us wary of crossing any threshold into a space where there's no obvious second exit.

One of John Saladino's pet phrases was, "Every chair needs a friend—and it's a table." It's how he illustrated the connectivity between décor and basic needs. He was stating a fact that's at once basic and profound—we all need nurturing environments where we're able to relax, daydream, nest, read, talk, or eat in peace. The true test of any designer is whether he or she is able to balance the complexities of human scale, practicality, and aesthetic composition within a tiny space. After that, progressing on to a grander scale is a piece of cake—every large room should simply be treated as a cluster of smaller rooms.

Often when designing, it's just as important to evaluate what's outside a room as inside. Some windows face a distant mountain range; some look directly into a neighbor's stairwell. A room might have the most glorious proportions and good bones, but its exterior view should also direct furniture placement. Nowadays, since Diana Vreeland's witty aphorism about the eye needing to travel has become a household phrase, most people appreciate the sentiment. If you are lucky enough to have a killer view, arrange the furniture in a way that encourages people to sit and look out at it. If you face a brick wall or a dark airshaft, liven up the interior with pieces interesting enough in their own right to draw attention away from it. And always remember that the difference between

a room filled with a variety of shapes, textures, colors, and styles and a room where all of its furniture is uniform in period, style, or provenance is the difference between a lively cocktail party and a museum.

When I'm ready to sketch layouts, I try to put myself into the same mindset of Symbolist poet Paul Valéry, who wrote that "to see is to forget the name of the thing one sees." I don't want any preconceptions to cloud my creative process, so I don't focus on a lamp or table's maker, period, or style. I don't differentiate between Aalto, IKEA, or rococo. I ignore the object-at-hand's monetary value. I try and maintain this state throughout the design process, and I find that it truly helps. An interior designer feels his or her work is complete at that indefinable point where there's simply nothing left to add and nothing seems to need to be taken away, and that harmony should be worked toward regardless of the perceived value of any one piece. I recently revisited an Upper West Side apartment I'd designed some time ago, and I noticed that a lineup of objects on a side table seemed to be off-kilter. It needed the balance of a small white object. From my perspective, an inexpensive ceramic tchotchke from CB2 would have done the trick, but the client resolved it differently—with an amazing Louise Bourgeois sculpture. My work sets the stage and gives direction, but it always leaves room for its owner to improvise.

LEFT Room-wide, bottom-up solar window shades shield the living room in a late-nineteenth-century Gramercy Park townhouse from sun glare and street activity. Simple, angular seating in dark, masculine colors offsets the elaborate historic molding. Wood wainscoting relates to the floor finishes and conceals the mechanicals for perimeter lighting that bathes the wall.

PREVIOUS PAGES Ornate plaster moldings and beautiful period doorways set the tone for the interior design's proportions, texture, and coloration. ABYU Lighting's tubular chandelier made from hand-cut plate glass wrapped in nickel wire references a 1960's Paco Rabanne dress and helps to ameliorate the dining room's lofty ceiling heights.

ABOVE An Art Deco chair from the client's collection sits to the left of the room's steel hearth. A side table displays a tumbleweed sculpture, providing an artful composition and supplying beauty for beauty's sake in a room otherwise devoid of wall art. RIGHT A mirror repurposed from the living room, where it was overshadowed by the abundance of other molding, was retrofitted with backlighting; its placement in a tiny powder room gives it a particularly grand presence. A stainless-steel pipe faucet originates in the floor and hovers above a black limestone sink; a sliding aluminum door conceals the room's other necessary fixtures. OVERLEAF An 8,000-square-foot Tribeca duplex with floor-to-ceiling windows on three sides and a wraparound terrace appears to float above the city, thanks to a lack of unnecessary interior walls and small furniture groupings with tailored, graphic silhouettes that create a series of 'rooms' and bring intimacy to an otherwise commercially scaled space.

ABOVE There are no privacy concerns in the spacious master bathroom—its window faces the Hudson River—so the transparent draperies serve only to soften sun glare. A Corian tub is stationed between opposing dual showerheads, and partner sinks flank the room's dry section. OPPOSITE, TOP A floor-to-ceiling wooden box sheathed in oak houses the apartment's mechanicals as well as a powder room where a one-way mirror looks onto an additional seating area that's anchored by an ornate Chinese bed. Draperies beyond keep the kitchen out of sight when not in use. OPPOSITE, BOTTOM LEFT One of the owners' more treasured pieces of art, an encaustic landscape of trees by Doug & Mike Starn, has pride of place in the kitchen. Bulthaup's smart-looking wood-and-aluminum cabinetry establishes a modern, industrial mood. OPPOSITE, BOTTOM RIGHT A plaster staircase's sculptural form is highlighted by a backlit wall and its clean, white surface contrasts with a short flight of steps and a central pillar built from French limestone. Its handrail is bronze piping. OVERLEAF A round carpet placed on top of a slate floor defines the perimeters of a family den. An ornate Chinese chamber bed contrasts with the deliberate playfulness in the exaggerated scale and shapes of Frank Gehry's Wiggle chair, Brunschwig & Fils's more serious leather armchair, and a giant wire-based floor lamp from Marset.

LEFT John Saladino first designed this timeless apartment, so a complete revamp seemed unnecessary, even after a period of many years had gone by. A sharpening of the old/new, smooth/rough, dark/light juxtapositions—achieved through new upholstery and the introduction of some whimsical, modern shapes—helped the original design remain relevant. ABOVE Toshiyuki Kita's Dodo recliner for Cassina remains sleek even when it shifts to horizontal. A floor-to-ceiling wall treatment of draperies hides several bookshelves and a TV screen, allowing the room to feel uncluttered and serene. PREVIOUS PAGES The walls, draperies, and ceiling in the living room of this 8,000-square-foot Upper East Side apartment are all a blue-tinged white and its floor is a light-colored oak, so the furniture appears to float in an airy shell. Several sofas—the smallish two-seaters were designed by John Saladino—radiate out from a central fireplace. The configuration is cozy for a lone person, but also easily accommodates a cocktail party for fifty.

LEFT John Saladino's classic Calla chairs in the dining area at one end of the living room received slipcovers to make them impervious to the owner's grandchildren, but the integrity of their arched seats and clean-lined silhouettes remains intact nevertheless. ABOVE The use of gold and silver leaf on the headboard in the master bedroom was inspired by an Italian rococo antique from The Bauers Hotel in Venice. The bedspread is constructed from two layers of Coraggio fabric—one transparent, one diaphanous—that have no memory retention for wrinkles. OVERLEAF Art should reflect the spirit of a home but never dominate it. This apartment in the Pierre Hotel was finished with a palette of oranges, rusts, and pinks that complement the client's modern art collection and give it much more context than white walls ever could.

PRIMERA
PLANTA

ABOVE I expanded my first weekend house in Amagansett from a trailer-sized 700 square feet to a marginally more respectable 1,100 square feet, and a highly composed interior laid out like a stage set helped to endow the small house with stature and dignity. Its seafoam-green monochromatic scheme echoed the color of the ocean. Similarly pine floors, doors, and built-ins matched the shade of beach sand tracked in on pleasant summer days. LEFT The master bedroom sat beyond the den; its bed was tucked into a bay window like a minuscule cubbyhole inside an already small room. Mosquito netting and draperies on three sides utilized low-budget Covington fabric that cost four dollars a yard at the time.

ABOVE Philippe Starck's original design for the Mondrian Hotel in Los Angeles is considered to be iconic, so a *Through the Looking Glass* theme—a natural sequel to his original *Alice In Wonderland* concept—felt respectful. A freestanding mirror in every standard room doubles as a television and can be rotated to be viewed in either the living or sleeping areas. LEFT In a penthouse suite, a chandelier composed of nine individual pendants makes a big bespoke impact on a deceptively low budget. Positioned to overlap the borders of a square table, it visually increases the size of the dining space. Shimmering polyester curtains play against silvery-gold walls to add to the sense of drama. OVERLEAF A large, rectangular living room in a 4,000-square-foot house in Palm Beach is a circulation hub for the entire first floor, so we designed three separate groupings of furniture to encourage conversation. Upholstered entirely in Rogers & Goffigon peach-colored linen, the room feels like a natural color-wheel counterpart to the lush green foliage just beyond the French doors.

ABOVE A chest of drawers with a Greek key–style motif from Liz O' Brien takes its color scheme from the swimming pool outside the master bedroom. A scrim of translucent voile floating behind the bed mimics the movement of wind across water and serves as the room's only artwork. LEFT Dining room chairs in two styles—dark wood or slipcovered with channeled fabric by Coraggio Textiles—relate to the two-dining-table setup of the room. Both allow for flexible seating arrangements. OVERLEAF The living room of a client who downsized into a Park Avenue apartment features several prototype John Saladino pieces. The dramatic window treatment—a translucent, room-width Roman blind behind a single, tied-back curtain—brings the classic pieces into a modern environment.

LEFT The living room's original brick-and-dark-wood fireplace surround was refreshed with marble and now displays a collection of celadon Chinese ceramics. A mix of antique Venetian chairs and inexpensive ceramic stools from West Elm sit near a Saladino tea table and on Chinese Khotan carpets from the client's extensive collection. ABOVE The den is used mainly at night, so wide draperies help to tone down the orange glow from a neighboring brick building. The shiny, pewter-finish wallpaper showcases a framed collection of vintage photographs of Venice. To keep the room's sight lines unobstructed, one elongated banquette spans an entire wall, the dining table was lowered, and an ottoman was introduced as an additional surface for trays and drinks.

LEFT A tight budget only afforded minimal interventions in a Park Avenue apartment, so the inherited Gracie wallpaper had to stay. Semitranslucent slipcovers for the backs of a set of Queen Anne dining chairs contain buttons and other dressmaker detailing inspired by Vera Wang wedding dresses. Along with tailored Roman shades, they offset the formality of the furniture and update the wall covering as well. ABOVE On either side of the entrance to the dining room, draperies—one translucent, the other wool with borders embroidered by Penn & Fletcher—delineate the transition from one space to another and diminish the impact of the highly graphic wallpaper.

ABOVE The living room's layout takes its lead from a stylized, centrally hung Cindy Sherman photograph. No two pieces of furniture here are in pairs or match, so the room's composition feels random and sculptural rather than pre-set. A curved sofa delineates the seating area and well-proportioned windows make the room feel aristocratic. RIGHT The mantel of an original wood fireplace surround in the library sits below a Nancy Corzine mirror that was inspired by a Giò Ponti design. A symmetrical lineup of candlesticks is an anchoring arrangement in a room where the client's collection of photographs constantly rotates and changes. FOLLOWING PAGES Photographer Mark Seliger's spacious loft, located in a former factory on New York's West Side Highway, has 12-foot-high ceilings. He wanted a diminutive Heywood-Wakefield desk to play a pivotal part in its layout; encasing it inside a 5-by-12-foot clear acrylic frame enhanced its presence substantially. Dark paint in the hall helps a collection of framed photographs stand out.

DAVID BAILEY
ISRAEL
TOM FORD
Self-Portrait
Thomas Ruff
BERT STERN
JOSEF SUDEK

OSCAR NIGHT · VANITY FAIR

UPON REFLECTION

Mirrors create volume, depth, and perspective in instant, nonsurgical ways. Appropriately sized and placed, they're hard to match for potency. They're even capable of injecting grandiosity into a cubbyhole. Whether a mirror leans or hangs, its frame is all-important. Slim, simple frames tend to give prominence to the reflection; thick, carved, and intricate frames qualify as beautiful objects in their own right, making what they reflect secondary. Rococo Venetian mirrors with wide, polished bevels and intricate rosettes are a particular favorite of mine. They come into their own when surrounded by a sea of angular shapes for contrast. Antique or tinted glass alters reality in gentle, forgiving ways so it's especially appealing in a bedroom, where it comes across as nostalgic and even romantic.

Remember that a mirror only comes to life once an observer confronts it. Position it where it's most useful. Where it reflects something intriguing, colorful, or memorable; where it captures movement; where it best scatters light. When an angled mirror reflects back something from beyond a direct line of sight—around a corner or into a second mirror, creating an infinite number of reflections—it can become playful, disarming, or hallucinatory.

I'm not a fan of overtly distorting, circular mirrors because their take is so myopic and my instincts are normally to open up space, but they serve a limited purpose. Convex bull's-eye mirrors date back to the Federal Era, where they often hung in dining rooms to allow servants to survey an entire table of guests at a glance. Concave mirrors, by contrast, focus light in a central point, producing a reflection where everything seems converged and almost telescopic. Speaking of geometric shapes, think twice before you hang a rectangular mirror horizontally. It's sure to widen a space, but it feels counterintuitive. Hanging it vertically will add a perception of height—always desirable.

A pool of still water or any polished surface also qualifies as a mirror. If it's prominent enough, a shiny ceiling can also rank as a room's animated fifth wall. Mirrored ceilings have kinky connotations, but I often line entire walls with plate glass when I feel the need to redefine spatial perspectives. Use the same device behind a recessed wall of shelves to add depth, height, and width.

Don't confine mirrors to the indoors. Think about attaching a mirror to a garden fence or a terrace wall where it can reflect flowers and shrubs, doubling the pleasure you obtain from them. Mirrors are also an effective cover for a low dividing wall between two balconies in a high-rise apartment building. It can turn one end of a veranda into a foliage-filled mural or double the amount of light seeping onto a screened-in porch.

CHAPTER 3

THEATRICAL MAGIC

Space is the ultimate luxury. The houses of my childhood in Puerto Rico felt enormous because they had several inner courtyards or because their gardens trailed onto endless stretches of sandy beach, but they were really just of average size. When we can't have space, the perception of space will do. I want the sense that more is always just around the corner to permeate my work, so I'm always challenging standard four-wall boundaries. I'm inspired by the mid-twentieth-century modernist architects whose houses obliterated the distinction between indoors and out, and like them I often find myself figuring out ways to make walls disappear or at least recede so they lose their prominence. I wouldn't call myself "demolition-happy," and I'm not a particular fan of open-plan living, I'm just a realist who likes to use a little sleight of hand now and then.

Geometry and psychology affect the way we perceive architecture. A room feels smaller to us when its sight lines from inside to out, from back to front, and from side to side are not addressed or resolved. And if the vista between interlocking spaces isn't coordinated, there is simply no way to evoke a sense of continuity. Harmony resulting from architectural seamlessness is transformative. It filters into our thought processes to instill a sense of calm, and it extends all of our horizons—literally and metaphorically.

When we think about claustrophobic spaces, small closets usually come to mind, but an illogical layout or unedited furnishings can also make even the largest rooms feel cramped. You can still bruise your shin on an awkwardly placed chair in a palace. Clutter is also psychologically restrictive. I can always detect an anxious tone in someone's voice when they refer to their belongings as "stuff." It means they have way too much.

Lighting is the easiest way to open up a tight area. You can take the direct route—simply plugging in a lamp or two—but you can also boost the perception of light in a room indirectly by a introducing a reflective surface or a lighter wall color. Black-and-white Hollywood movies from the 1920s and 1930s are master classes in graphic lighting. Back then, set designers had to be inventive because the era's single-lens cameras compressed and flattened everything. Strategically placed light sources were the only way to help sets acquire some dimension.

Pumping up the intensity or scale of one element in a tiny space lends it some bravura and turns a lack of size into a witty attribute. A large rococo chandelier or high-octane patterned wallpaper throw off all our preconceived notions of relativity in a windowless powder room. Highly textural Venetian plaster in an outrageous color lining a short, nondescript hall turns a mundane passageway into something much more memorable.

Color has magical qualities. It's a mind-altering wizard. A tiny, narrow room appears to widen when both its shorter walls are painted a shade or two darker than its longer walls. And minus adding actual real estate, the best way to make a room feel generous is to give it the impression of height or depth. The eye considers a symmetrically proportioned room to be bigger than it actually is.

Square rooms are generally thought to be restful, but we all respond to forms differently, so consider how you respond to shapes and if you know that you enjoy one over another, work to incorporate it. Some people are visually soothed by the lyrical curve of a camelback sofa or the pleasing lines of an orthogonal Donald Judd desk. Somewhere in my early life, for example, circles resonated for me. Now they're a leitmotif in all my projects. I mean, we instinctively huddle around a campfire—we don't form a square! Symbolically, circles represent unity or an autonomous whole. A round rug has an incomparable ability to anchor a coffee table, a couple of armchairs, and a sofa. A circle also suggests a loop of successive movement, so when a round carpet sits on a dark, square floor it and everything placed upon it practically levitates.

All this is not to say that rooms should seem airy at the expense of coziness. Our individual notions of comfort are also linked to early conditioning, so they're just as subjective. We're tightly swaddled in a blanket as soon as we leave our mother's wombs, so we associate safety and protection with tactile things that envelop us. Some people enjoy reclining in a deep-seated wing-back chair or wrapping themselves in an angora throw. Add thoughtful comforts to every space.

The most alluring spaces appeal to all the senses—as retailers know all too well. Chefs are some of my favorite role models because they consider taste, sound, sight, and smell in every dish they prepare. Adding small sensory touches to a room also increases our psychological perception of how welcoming or spacious it seems to be. Music is always playing in a spa, hotel, or boutique, isn't it? In more haunting ways incense, aromatic flowers and perfumed candles are potent reminders of a space and we carry traces of their scent in our clothing or on our belongings so they're with us long after we leave someone's house. Appealing to all the senses is the best way to make a space memorable. Illusionists know that distracting us makes us see what they want us to—not what actually is.

PREVIOUS PAGES The design of beauty expert Tracie Martyn's salon in Manhattan wows clients with experiential color, not to mention a room full of golden Buddha statues. A private area—configured as a living room and semiconcealed behind sheer drapes—where she holds pre-treatment chats exemplifies her intimate, nonclinical approach. LEFT Humidifiers stimulate the air with aroma-infused clouds along a hallway that leads to several chromatherapy treatment rooms. Its purple walls and ceiling utilize a color that's reputedly meditative, transformational, and healing. ABOVE Imperfections and patina on the floors and furniture send a positive, subliminal message about Martyn's respect for the aging process. Shafts of sunlight that flood through a windowed skylight in a sitting area activate faceted Swarovski crystals that stud a wall. OVERLEAF In the carpet-free waiting room, an assortment of comfortable seating celebrates diversity. Curtains hung 12 inches in from the wall delay the transmission of harsh, western light and turn views of weathered buildings on Fifth Avenue into subtle mirages. An ABYU floor lamp made up of two shades—feathers layered beneath a transparent drum—conveys a "beauty's-only-skin-deep" message.

THE ART OF YOGA

NOW!

LEFT Performance is a leitmotif in music producer, actor, and entrepreneur Sean Combs's apartment on Fifty-seventh Street and Broadway. Sheer black draperies, reflective silvery ceilings and walls, and a see-through baby grand piano epitomize cool glamour. ABOVE During the day, wraparound windows provide views of Central Park; nighttime vistas celebrate a light-filled skyline that make the apartment itself entertainment. Plexiglas furniture—including a low sofa base designed to align with the window mullions—never obscures, upstages, or interferes with the exterior views.

ABOVE A media center features a screen the size of a small movie theater's. A collection of photographs taken by the legendary Gordon Parks hangs in prominent places throughout the apartment. RIGHT Combs tends to be a night owl, so all the windows are fitted with blackout shades. One of the building's structural columns is sheathed in illuminated glass, making it essentially a floor-up chandelier. Highly reflective ceilings present yet another animated surface in the apartment as they record shadowy traces of headlights and neon signs. Every room has a black-and-white color scheme, lending the space a pervading sense of Hollywood-heyday nostalgia.

LEFT Fiestaware ceramics inspired the array of colors in a sixth-floor Belle Island apartment I formerly owned in Miami. Some spaces, like the dining room, contained furniture prototypes I was trying to resolve—comfort wasn't of the utmost importance. Mirrored walls brought in views of the bay and reflected multicolored interior paint treatments, making the atmosphere surreal. ABOVE The intensity of light in Miami makes saturated color pop, so bold combinations feel perfectly harmonious. In this case, orange progressed to yellow and then to aqua en route from the master bedroom to the hallway.

ABOVE A platform bed installed against a bank of windows and featuring plenty of built-in storage resembles a bunk on an ocean liner. Mirrored surfaces that act as a headboard and footboard introduce a sense of spaciousness; curtains close off visual access to the living room. OPPOSITE, ABOVE A home office is easily secluded from the apartment's aqua-blue entry via a bank of white draperies. Butternut squash–colored walls and wood Venetian blinds tempered the sunlight and helped it rank as the apartment's most tranquil space. OPPOSITE, BELOW The living room gives a nod to classic Miami sun porches with wraparound casement windows and a mix of modern and rattan furniture on a woven Moroccan carpet. In this room as elsewhere in the apartment, the saturation of color plays off against the dramatic blue skies visible outside the windows.

Lavish amounts of purplish taupe and gray play with perspective in fashion designer Steve Fabrikant's small design studio on East Fifth-eighth Street in Manhattan. A Noguchi paper lamp, leather-upholstered hospital seat, and a modular chair covered in pony skin deviate from the monochromatic shell created from matte Benjamin Moore paint and two Gretchen Bellinger fabrics.

LEFT At the curtained kitchen entrance, a strategically placed leather chair picked up at a Paris flea market teams up with high candlesticks and full floor-to-ceiling curtains covering all the interior doors to create strong vertical lines, employing a legerdemain that implies the space is far larger than its actual 500 square feet. ABOVE a work/dining table sits adjacent to a set of silvery gray draperies that hides the living room. The whole space makes a statement about color and serves as an enveloping environment for Fabrikant to meet buyers, fit models, and sketch. Last but not least, it's a flattering showroom for his style of clothing.

ABOVE Fabrikant lives in a 2,500-square-foot apartment adjacent to the studio; this space is dressed in a calming palette of taupe, gold, and cream. Brocade upholstery; a low, freestanding screen embracing two armchairs; and a large leaning mirror reflecting a wide, molding-free, enfilade create a sense of formality. RIGHT In the southern-facing dining room, two types of chairs—with and without slipcovers—sit around a cabriole-legged Biedermeier table. Thick, art-free walls house discreetly hidden storage compartments and a wide-plank parquet floor underscores the scale of the room.

PREVIOUS PAGES An uptown Riverside Drive apartment in Manhattan emanates the attitude of an open downtown loft thanks to a spacious living room and an angled seating arrangement. Chairs designed by Walter Gropius and lacquered in car paint are intended to feel nomadic. When moved from one area to another, their saturated colors reinvigorate the space's predominantly neutral shell. The antique dining room chandelier mimics palm fronds for a touch of whimsy. LEFT A gold, 10-by-6-foot oval ceiling tray passively creates flow between the entry, living room, and library. Sandblasted aluminum-and-frosted-glass sliding doors resemble shoji screens. A 6-inch-wide, turquoise-tinted mirror is a Feng Shui solution that gives immediacy to a set of bedrooms at the end of a long corridor.

ABOVE A small, bright-red kitchen packs glamour and attitude. Cabinets feature a stenciled, lacquered Fortuny pattern; the backsplash is mirrored. Glass mesh that sheathes the lit range hood is deceptively functional: it detaches and can be folded easily to fit into a dishwasher.

Mexican author Laura Esquivel's 800-square-foot duplex in Greenwich Village required a little sleight-of-hand to overcome its geometric constrictions. The visual elimination of sharp corners insinuates areas exist that aren't actually there, for example. In the main room, a pentagon-shaped floor plan situates the kitchen—an important space for the author of *Like Water For Chocolate*—at its flattest part.

LEFT A pair of fuchsia—or *rosa mexicano*—painted columns flank the breakfast counter. One is structural, the other purely decorative; the addition fools people in the sitting area into thinking it's rectangular. Esquivel, a prolific cook, took advantage of the hardware and molding-free kitchen cabinets by hanging pots and pans from their doors. ABOVE In a sitting area opposite the main entrance on the second floor, a smooth lavender wall, counter, and chair interact with the room's northern light. Paradoxically, the triangular-shaped counter works to echo and diminish the room's triangular shape.

ABOVE A few steps beyond the bedroom, a former terrace functions as Esquivel's study and writing area. The glass-and-metal roof brings in amazing amounts of light even on the grayest of days. RIGHT A prominently angled wall kept the master bathroom from accommodating both a tub and shower—until the space was reconfigured to house them together behind a see-through shower curtain. Light streams in from a south-facing window and inexpensive 1-inch-square ceramic tiles line the walls and form a raised lip division between the wet and dry areas, giving the small room an airy, bespoke feeling.

LIGHT FANTASTIC

Light is a palpable entity. When you step inside a weighty Gothic cathedral, for example, its rose and stained-glass windows make the entire nave vibrate with emotion. Light's animating force always affects and augments how we process color. Living or working in a naturally lit environment is gentler on the eyes—and therefore makes us more productive and content—so the Holy Grail of interior design is being able to simulate lighting conditions that mimic the sun's warmth and optimism. My favorite lighting cocktail mixes incandescent, LED, and even fluorescent bulbs because the three play off each other and compensate for each other's deficiencies.

I don't often define hard-and-fast rules, but there are some where lighting scenarios are concerned. A lone, glaring ceiling fixture serves a utilitarian purpose in a garage, but it leaves a lot to be desired in any living space. A solitary chandelier only works in a dining room if it's lit in tandem with sconces or candles—and always put its bulb on a dimmer and suspend it at a height where it won't throw shadows onto the faces of seated guests. Use an assortment of sconces and standing and table lamps to create uniform light throughout a room, but install them so their bulbs sit at a similar height on the same horizontal plane. No one should ever be viewed in penumbra.

Sometimes I use three types of fixtures adjacent to seating: overhead or ambient fixtures to illuminate generally; a task lamp on a side table, to highlight specific activities; and a whimsical lamp as a just-for-the-fun-of-it mood enhancer. Lovers of tradition tend to favor pairs of lamps throughout a project but that's too predictable for my taste, even in the most symmetrical of scenarios like on either side of a bed. My advice about bedside fixtures is to install a task and a whimsical lamp on each nightstand. Unless you have nightstands that don't match, then use paired fixtures for the sake of consistency. If the nightstands are identical, mismatch the lamps but make sure they're roughly the same height. Avoid wall-mounted, swing-arm lamps—they're almost impossible to angle correctly.

Always keep exterior lighting subtle so it won't drown out the night sky. No one wants to be blinded by a glaring fixture in a garden or on a porch. Outdoor lights should be powerful enough to illuminate a pathway but also leave the eye able to easily adjust to the glow of the moon and stars.

CHAPTER 4

STAYING ON SCRIPT

Our home is a natural extension of our personality. It expresses our concepts of happiness, beauty, comfort, and hospitality; it echoes our desires and aspirations; it documents our travels; it reveals our family mythology and ancestry. I take time to get to know my clients intimately because their personal story is always my first inspiration for their décor. I often rely on it as a basis for a loose theme that then becomes a working tool for all of us in the studio and keeps us on script. If you think of an interior like a work of theater, the individual actors—color, art, furnishings, finishes—work together to produce an engaging and satisfying overall narrative.

The infallible Billy Baldwin said, "The worst thing any decorator can do is give a client the feeling that he's walking around somebody else's house." That's an eternal truth. Every room needs to belong to its owner on a visceral level. Happily, technology can now help me get to know my clients very well. I ask a slew of basic lifestyle questions as we're getting started, of course, but then I set them up with a simple Pinterest page. That website mimics what I've been doing for years when I clip an article from a travel magazine or save a postcard, fragment of embroidery, or a coaster from a cocktail bar. These pages don't need to have any logical sense of organization, and I never judge them as good or bad. I distill the random imagery—a celebrity, place, tool, animal, fabric, fruit, typeface, concept, building or hairdo—into a design vocabulary. Then I begin to sketch out my ideas and create storyboards from fabric swatches, paint chips, and flooring samples. Once in a while a client takes credit for a project I've designed and I find it perversely flattering. It means they truly relate to the story their home tells, and that's the ultimate goal.

I've heard stories of clients who ask their designer to reproduce an interior verbatim from the pages of a shelter magazine, but I don't see any virtue in appropriating someone else's style—you'll never feel comfortable living there. A client once showed me an article about a house she coveted, but after we analyzed it we realized she was more drawn to the general "feeling" its colors, furnishings, and art evoked than to its actual architecture. We used that discussion as a springboard to develop her own unique style. Another client recently requested a dining table for twelve because he is drawn to formal spaces—I reminded him that he rarely entertains and hates to cook, so we compromised on a more realistic option. Function should always drive form where homes are concerned.

My apartment is within walking distance of Manhattan's major galleries, so I spend a lot of time in them gathering inspiration. Even though art certainly influences my work and asking clients about their taste in art helps me to get to know their aesthetic sense quickly, I rarely buy paintings, photography, or sculpture for my projects. Many of my clients tend to have their own fleshed-out collections, but more important, I don't think of art as a merely decorative element. I see it as a visualization of our internalized philosophy. It's in a different league from furniture. It shouldn't be purchased to match a sofa color or the period of a bureau. It should be acquired because it speaks to you.

I dress and live casually. I know designers who take the pursuit of objectivity to extremes by separating their professional and personal styles completely, but that would be too much of a dichotomy for me to handle. If I'm hired to work for a client who has a formal lifestyle, I always recommend a few aesthetic twists here and there to keep rooms from taking themselves too seriously. I could never do strictly traditional restorations even though I have classical training; as a modernist, I find I have to practice what I preach. Formality—in people as well as interiors—is deadly if it comes off as stuffy. There's a big difference between precious and pretentious rooms. It's important to find approachable, noncliché ways to present invaluable artwork or museum-quality antiques. It is possible to satisfy tradition and still provide comfort for every member of the family—including children and pets.

Defining a style for a corporate project is, in some ways, even more challenging than trying to physically translate an individual personality into the form of an interior. Hotel design, for example, involves broader concepts and themes—a more overarching story, if you will. There, I need to appeal to a predetermined demographic—a cultural tribe, a generation, or a professional group. Any accessories I choose must be gender neutral and the beds, tables, chairs, and stools need to conform to a wide range of body types, aesthetic sensibilities, and ages. Some hospitality designers try to create a "home away from home," but I know that whenever I stay at a hotel, I want the tangible comfort you do get at home—AND the luxuries you can't get at home. Along with the down pillows and attentive room service I crave a certain amount of glamour and theatricality that I couldn't live with 24/7 so I feel as though I've done something eventful. The goal of creating a space that feels intuitive and honest is the same for a hotel as for a home, but let's face it: when you're paying for a night out you want to be dazzled and entertained.

PREVIOUS PAGES The erotic symbolism that runs throughout Jean Cocteau's 1946 film *La Belle et la Bête* inspired the interiors of the Soho Mondrian Hotel in New York. In Cocteau's grown-up fairy tale, image sequences bleed into mirrors so the hotel's blue lobby reproduces itself in a reflective blue wall. Metal furniture finishes allude to the jewelry the Beast gave Belle; stools have animal-shaped feet, and the stenciled ceiling references a rose stolen from the Beast's creeper-wreathed castle garden. LEFT A 30-foot-high, pitched-glass ceiling makes a spacious communal dining room adjacent to the lobby feel like a hybrid of ballroom and greenhouse. Green walls, lacquered wood, wicker, and blue-painted metal chairs gather beneath a battalion of crystal chandeliers and amid fern-filled planters and potted trees.

ABOVE Dinner guests eat in close proximity to art in the form of an enormous, 32-foot-long sculpture by Beth Lipman, who often uses clear glass to explore symbolism in her work.

this is not a brothel
there are
no prostitutes
at this address

LEFT Mister H, a speakeasy-style club in the hotel, features lacquered red walls, red acrylic lanterns, and a salon-style arrangement of mirrors. Guests arrive through a nondescript, unmarked door on the Chinatown side of the building. A fog machine envelops the floor at night and enhances the space's calculatedly seedy environment. ABOVE An 11-foot-high, curved wall guides guests through the hotel's city-block-long lobby. Decorative elements relate back to the storyline—the wall studs reference sturdy castle architecture, and Swarovski crystals used throughout the space allude to how Belle's tears turned into diamonds when she wept.

TOP, ABOVE Stunning views of downtown Manhattan obviate the need for art in each of the hotel's 270 guest rooms. A crisp white-and-Wedgwood-blue color scheme for the décor references Belle's blue dress and gave us a licensed guide for the upholstery. ABOVE Opposite each headboard, a panel of smoky blue glass continues the fantastical storyline established in the lobby. Rather than run-of-the-mill table lamps, custom-designed floating sconces flank each stack of bed pillows. OPPOSITE Like most of Manhattan's boutique hotels, the Mondrian's standard rooms are extremely compact, so furnishings are expected to do double duty. Here, a sink sits on top of a marble counter above a concealed refrigerator that moonlights as a bar.

(MALIN+GOETZ)

LEFT An eighteenth-century Francesco Beda print I found in a Virginia flea market was enlarged to occupy more than half of a tiny storefront's main wall in Manhattan's Greenwich Village. The space was originally conceived as a temporary pop-up store for Diptyque candles, but thanks to its success the company kept it open for three years. ABOVE The brand's black-and-white packaging and logo stood out when juxtaposed against the mural's soft lines and colors. The fire department banned real flames in the space, so a lineup of flickering monitors replicated the hypnotic glow of lit *bougies* and each candle's fragrance could be tested by a sprayed sample.

PREVIOUS PAGES A Rockaway, Queens, apartment where my husband and I unwind on the weekends has a tongue-in-cheek theme: the informal retreat for a young Marie Antoinette. Her portrait reigns supreme in the living room and floats in an acrylic frame on top of walls painted a Tiffany blue. LEFT On a glass-enclosed balcony, a circular table, vintage ice-cream-parlor chairs, and a Charles Eames fiberglass rocker make it my favorite place to dine. The double-height space is also a perfect sleeping porch and a decompression spot for gazing at the horizon. ABOVE Everything in the 1,000-square-foot apartment is lighthearted, including a taxidermy rooster who greets guests and points them toward a 180-degree view of the Atlantic Ocean. OVERLEAF, LEFT A play on the most gender-associated color—pink—is punctuated by a plush, wall-mounted teddy bear artist Mattia Biagi dipped in tar. A La Murrina glass chandelier, dyed Mongolian-lamb bedspread, customized bedding from Nancy Koltes, and curtains tailored by Kenny Flam create a monochromatic space accented with black-and-white pillows depicting Tom of Finland illustrations. OVERLEAF, RIGHT A den/guest bedroom holds a low recamier from 145 Antiques. Diaphanous white curtains temper afternoon light. The candlesticks are by Ted Muehling, the table is a prototype for the Mondrian L.A., and I designed the wing-back chair for the Mondrian Scottsdale.

glimmering gone
MUSEUM OF GLASS

Suna No Onna
Benjamin Noriega Ortiz

LEFT Dennis Freedman, the creative director of Barney's New York, commissioned me to design a conceptual display for a Balenciaga gown. My inspiration came from *Suna No Onna*, or *Woman in the Dunes*, a 1964 movie directed by Hiroshi Teshigahara. Three elements from this surreal tale of morality filled a Madison Avenue window: a monumental pile of sand, a feather lamp that references a crow, and mirrors that symbolize water. ABOVE Rhett Butler, the owner of E. R. Butler Hardware, thinks of his highly visible showroom windows on Prince Street in Soho as space for conceptual displays. Using ABYU feather shades, I condensed the story of *Swan Lake* into four scenarios, each starring a black or white incarnation of the bird.

An 8,000-square-foot duplex penthouse for performer/songwriter and interior designer Lenny Kravitz at 30 Crosby Street was conceived as a sophisticated-yet-fun, interactive palace. A Perspex swing hangs from the ceiling and greets guests in the otherwise traditionally appointed entrance lobby.

LEFT A Lucite baby grand piano formerly owned by the celebrated Swedish film director Ingmar Bergman was the first piece of furniture purchased for this project. An offbeat reinvention of a classic, it stylistically epitomizes the visual tone Kravitz wanted to achieve.

ABOVE An undulating wall snaking through the main living room derives its curved shape from the mass of building mechanicals it conceals. A cuff of beads and fur update a standing lamp Kravitz owned, and a plexiglass-legged chair pays homage to a Paul McCobb classic. The Jean Royère armchairs came from Maison Gerard.

LEFT, ABOVE A steep glass staircase with a glass railing and carpeted treads unites two interior floors. Its doppelganger, visible through glass walls, extends an outdoor space up onto a roof terrace. RIGHT, ABOVE An Art Deco table mounted on stone pedestals from Bernd Goeckler Antiques is a foil for a Jean-Michel Basquiat painting in a dining area. RIGHT An undulating wall was originally designed to have flames along its full length; when it radiated far too much heat, the fire pit was reduced to 4 feet. OPPOSITE, ABOVE A quartet of Andy Warhol portraits of Muhammad Ali sits above a Fortuny-covered Knoll sofa from George Smith. OPPOSITE, BOTTOM LEFT A screening room beyond one of many sitting rooms features draperies dripping with Swarovski crystals. OPPOSITE, BOTTOM RIGHT Water pours into a custom cement tub from the mouth of a sculpted plaster figure in an inversion of typical garden-fountain treatments.

A 15-by-10-foot panel of softly illuminated draperies defines a stagelike area as a living room. A pair of lamps—one positioned on a light box, the other on a table draped in silver leather—further defines the boundaries of the space. A Louis chair from Bernd Goeckler Antiques looks onto a cork Paul Frankl coffee table alongside leather-and-wool upholstered seating.

LEFT A Soho pop-up shop for Cartier, the venerable Parisian jeweler, was designed to launch a line of tiaras, bracelets, necklaces, and earrings called Délices. I took the literal translation of the word—delight, joy, fun—and filled the entire space with orange-colored candy a few shades removed from the company's signature crimson. Lollipops mounted in concentric circles and bags of candy tied with French ribbon served as decorative "artwork." ABOVE Piled high with a mountain of cellophane-wrapped sweets, the window overlooking the street was a tribute to the Cuban artist Félix González-Torres, who often created edible artwork.

ABOVE A rectangular wall mosaic composed of candied almonds resembled grotto-esque seashell art. It housed a screen playing looped videos of the detailed handiwork and craftsmanship that distinguishes the house's jewelry, which sat directly in front in a glass display case. RIGHT To counterbalance the space's immense amounts of vibrant color, vases full of white sugar cubes occupied illuminated, recessed niches. Cartier's desire to commit wholeheartedly to the candy concept meant that over 60 percent of the store's interior had nothing whatsoever to do with jewelry displays.

ENCORE

Subconsciously, we register low levels of stress if the layout of our immediate surroundings isn't clear. We're prone to a general feeling of subtle unease if we're not sure what we face on the other side of a partition; it's unsettling to not know what lies beyond a doorway. This is particularly true for public spaces like hotels, restaurants, department stores, and offices, but it also applies to residences.

When aspects of a design are repeated at intervals, a cavernous space loses some of its mystery. It's strange to think of sconces as confidence boosters, but it's reassuring when a series of them enables us to estimate a long corridor's length in one quick glance. It's comforting when all the windows of a villa wear the same stripy awning. Visual alliteration achieves the same results as its literary counterpart: it's emphatic, it's an aide-mémoire, and it constitutes a pattern.

Of course a room's architecture satisfies our basic need for order best, which is why Louis I. Kahn instructed his students to build projects where "the rooms have spoken to each other." A familiar motif—a reoccurring window shape, wall texture, light switch, window textile, or floor tile—emphasizes structural harmony so the whole feels melodic. Maybe it's also why Goethe referred to architecture as "petrified music." These kinds of aesthetic organizational clues are particularly helpful in a hotel, where they subliminally instill guests with navigational confidence. They're as much of an orientation device as the proverbial trail of breadcrumbs through a forest.

Harmony within each room and from room to room is just as psychologically important as harmony in an overall structure. Painting walls with incarnations of the same color is a simple way to establish an even flow throughout a house or an apartment. Hues with similar undertones also feel thematic—in a far less obvious way than a hit of the same bright color reverberating between a piece of art, a rug, a curtain, and then a pillow. Constructing all the cabinetry from one felled tree, or standardizing all the kick-plate and backsplash heights unifies a kitchen and actually makes it feel larger, for example. Randomness has the opposite effect. If every piece of hardware in a bathroom has a different finish—graphite, brass, and polished chrome—it's disquieting.

Too many echoing elements can have an unappealing effect as well. En masse they lose their conviction, particularly in a small space. If their use feels heavy-handed or nonstrategic, the perception of space decreases. Then repetition reads as redundancy; it stands for excess rather than access.

CHAPTER 5

MISE-EN-SCÈNE

While my childhood friends busied themselves with Legos and miniature cars, I was studiously rethinking our house's floor plan and our rooms' layouts. As I approached my early teens, my hobby took a more physical form: I decided I was ready to express myself in three dimensions. So I emptied my bedroom of all its books, gadgets, lamps, and furniture and painted all the remaining surfaces white. I polished the black terrazzo floor and delineated all the wall edges with one-inch-thick red tape. I asked my mother to sew me a coordinating coverlet for my mattress—white with welted red seams—and once my bed was parked centrally at a particular, askew angle it practically hovered in the room. In retrospect my creation was pretty radical for a teenage boy. As an adult, I realize it could have been a stage set for an existential play about containment. Luckily I had an understanding family who took my atypical behavior in stride. Then as now, I love to use provoking design, and still I find that one of the simplest but most arresting treatments is to create an all-white space.

White is the equivalent of a visual mantra to me. It levels me. It helps me regain a state of aesthetic equilibrium. Every day, all day I look at and handle wood and metal surfaces, plumbing fixtures, draperies, and flooring, so it's important that I come home to a cleansing environment that neutralizes, refreshes, and reinvigorates my eye. The Manhattan duplex I share with my husband, Steven Wine, is done exclusively in various rich shades of white. Our apartment's ceilings, walls and woodwork are all different intensities of cream. The gradual tonal shift between different elements creates a textural whole. It's all white, but no surface is *simply* white. In one corner it tinges green as light hits a nearby vase of tropical leaves; in another it blushes after it picks up red tones from a ceramic bowl; elsewhere it recedes and showcases the graphic, dark silhouette of a midcentury lamp. White is anything but a passive, noncommittal color. It even makes beige come alive.

In a real estate listing, our apartment would read like a conventional house: it has two floors, a staircase, a fireplace, a guest bedroom, a spacious kitchen, and lots of outdoor space. But it's anything but prosaic. All the walls and ceilings are finished with Venetian plaster—its embedded specks of mica act as miniature light receptors. Our white terrazzo entrance floor leads to wall-to-wall shag carpeting throughout; its texture and fuzziness dispel the cliché of white as a cool surface, at least underfoot. People assume living in a white environment must be a sanitizing experience, but to us it's the opposite. It sensitizes us. Although I can understand how some people may look on our setup as some kind of fantasy about living immaculately. Another criticism I've heard is that it's impractical. Dirt is a concern, but I addressed it by installing a washer and dryer right next to the entry door—the moment we walk in, we shed our city garb and change into "inside clothes." All of our upholstery is slipcovered. I am a pragmatist, and I know that spills happen. Though I'll confess that I do also keep a stockpile of bleach and Windex on hand.

Light and space artist James Turrell has said that "If the color is in the paint on the wall, then in making a structure and allowing light to enter it, the color will tend to ride on the walls. But if the color of the wall is white…color has the possibility of inhabiting the space [by riding on the light] and holding that volume rather than being on the wall." I couldn't agree more. I use white as frequently as I do because nothing else obliterates boundaries, opens our perceptions, and defines forms with such clarity. It absorbs any distractions it encounters and reduces them to an interplay of light and shadows. And while it neutralizes visual complexity it elevates the ordinary. It's also universally flattering. Young or old, we all look good in a crisp white shirt. The preferred background for every genre of portrait photographer is a roll of white seamless paper. Chefs know unadorned white china enhances the presentation of every dish. Color, whether primary or pastel, creates an optical diversion by calling attention to itself.

This pristine color definitely isn't for everyone. Very early in my career, after a magazine article showcased an all-white beach house I'd designed, I received a call from a woman who wanted something similar. I read a lot into a person's clothing, and during our first meeting I noticed that she was wearing a bright, patterned outfit. It seemed to match her vibrant personality, and it flattered her physically. I had a hard time imagining her living in a space devoid of saturated tones, but I shelved my misgivings because she was enthusiastic about the prospect of her new, white life. When I subsequently presented her with a gorgeous series of snowy storyboards, her expression told me she knew she'd commissioned far too extreme a look. Within minutes, she started to cry. Needless to say we backtracked and gradually introduced color until it accurately reflected her personality. Our preference for one color over another can't be taught. It's not a cerebral choice. It's a visceral, emotional response.

RUCE WEBER

PREVIOUS PAGES A weather-encrusted oyster shell with an iridescent interior is an apt analogy for this dark-shingled Hamptons house and its brilliant-white interiors. A formal dining room is mainly inhabited at night, but during the day a Hunter Douglas window shade transforms a nondescript view into a glowing light wall. LEFT These clients have an aversion to lamps and visible wiring, so in the 20-foot-high living room a quartet of four acrylic "light columns" illuminate and define perimeters at once. Doors to second-floor guest bedrooms sit behind the balcony's glass railing, designed by project architect Brian Boyle as a nonintrusive viewing platform over the space below.

ABOVE Views on three sides of the master bedroom look onto the garden, a hot tub, and a terrace. Several French doors concealed behind a wall of draperies open to convert the room into a sleeping porch. Jerusalem-stone floors that run throughout the space transition to wood in the sleeping quarters—both materials match the sand on nearby stretches of beach. RIGHT Accordion doors can stack open, making the pool an extension of the master bedroom's sitting room. Without a discernible demarcation between indoors and out, the architecture takes on the characteristics of a pavilion.

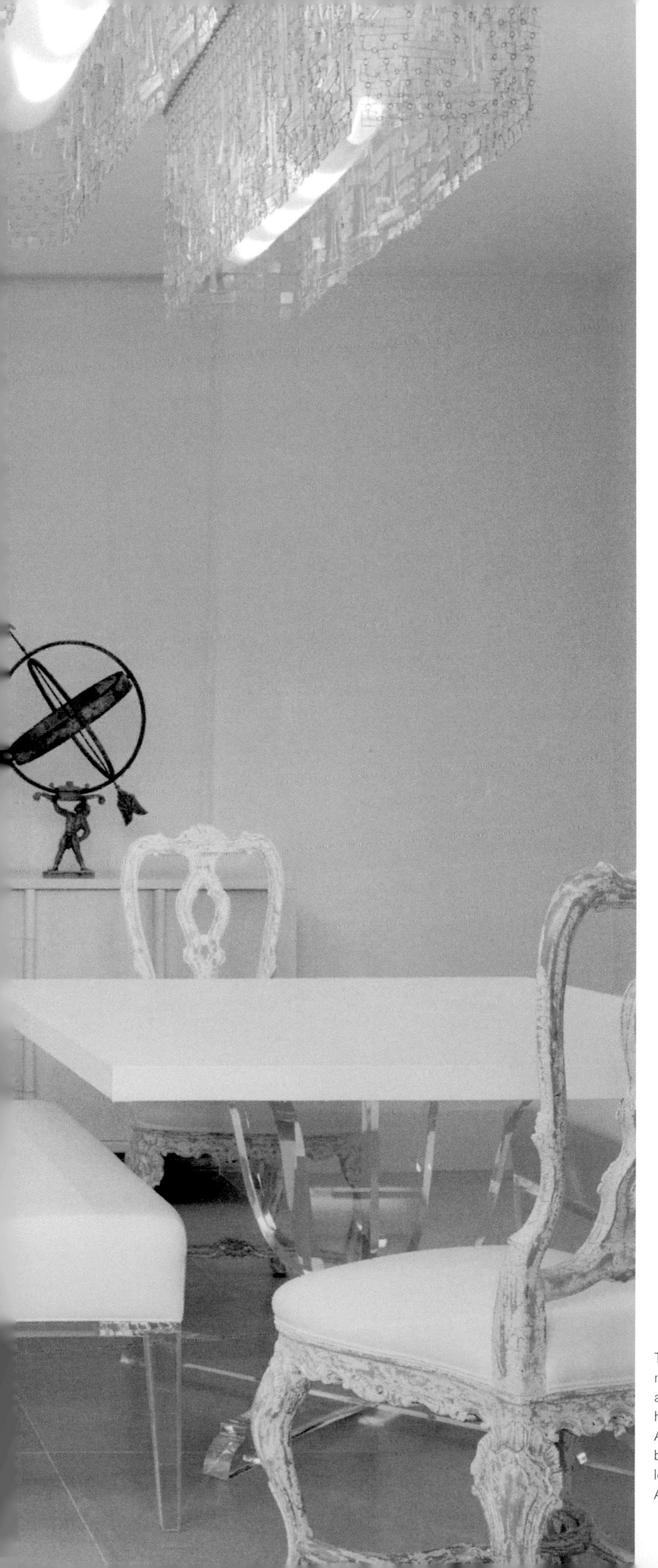

The dining room's two tables have no fixed abode—they reconfigure according to the number of guests to host a party of sixteen people, or two. Acrylic bases give the room's furniture buoyancy and prevent the numerous legs from attracting all the attention. A chandelier designed by Thomas Thompson and ABYU out of mesh and fiberglass radiates symmetrically from the ceiling's center. A palest-green organza scrim, hung an inch away from the wall above three 1950s cabinets, muffles sound.

FAR LEFT When filled with water, clear vases of mixed size and proportion become an intensely sculptural vehicle for light. LEFT In the living room, a rectangular artwork—a former window display depicting a sailboat—mirrors the proportions of a fireplace on an opposite wall to visually unite both ends of the room. LEFT, ABOVE During the summer months, the chain-mail guard on a black firebox is drawn back to house a plaster bust. Boxy chairs continue the space's strongly geometric vocabulary. RIGHT, ABOVE Surfaces in an all-white kitchen include acrylic cabinetry fronts and Caesarstone quartz counters that are impervious to stains. Both surfaces help draw light into one of the house's darker spaces.

PARIS LIVING ROOMS

PREVIOUS PAGES In a 1,000-square-foot Paris pied-à-terre, the white color scheme is deliberately low-maintenance. In the living room all the upholstery materials, from leather to Mongolian fur, can be easily spot-cleaned or washed. Mirrored tables reflect views of the Seine and Notre Dame. ABOVE The clients rarely cook, so a simple kitchen at the end of the entry hall suffices. It contains chairs picked up at Porte de Vanves flea market and a modern steel-and-glass table. White walls are tinged pink in the cast from a glass chandelier. RIGHT In the hall, a French blue tray ceiling conceals lighting and mediates the narrow passageway's height to keep it from feeling confining. FAR RIGHT The bedroom's walls are a warm, paper-bag color but white still plays a thematic role, down to a black-and-white photograph's frame. A closet full of clothing recedes behind a bank of double-width cotton draperies.

PREVIOUS PAGES A pristine-but-serviceable white interior for a 10,000-square-foot beach house in Quogue, New York, flatters an extensive collection of modern art. In the living room, upholstery fabrics—quilted, cotton, or vinyl—are all zippered for easy cleaning. Oval tables fabricated by Alpha Craft are custom designed; lamps sprouting out of them are by Jaime Hayon for Metalarte. LEFT In an Alpha Craft kitchen, a thick length of Corian wraps itself around an island. Above-counter cabinets studded with Swarovski crystals open up to sky-blue shelving inside. Benches and upholstered versions of Mexican barrel chairs surround a pair of dining tables. Orange teak cabinets store all the essentials for dining on a terrace facing the ocean. RIGHT Barnes Coy Architects kept customized aluminum window mullions thin to let in unobstructed ocean vistas. A table for two occupies a corner of the dining area in the kitchen.

ABOVE An 8-foot-wide bed dominates the master suite, where the full family often gathers to watch movies on a flat monitor suspended from a glass wall in front of a terrace. A clown diptych by artist Roni Horn hangs directly above the headboard. RIGHT The master suite's walk-in closet appears to be twice its actual size thanks to a 10-by-12-foot mirrored wall. Subtly concealed lighting and rippling curtains constructed by Flam Associates from RoseBrand theatrical fabric give neatly kept wardrobes, shelves, and cubbyholes an ethereal quality. A vitrine-topped cabinet provides easy access to jewelry.

LEFT In a guest bedroom, a large repurposed chandelier with wiring concealed by a silk sleeve hangs above an illuminated table. The headboard spans the entire room and is covered in patent vinyl. The bedspread is made from Nancy Koltes quilted cotton; draperies cut from dove-gray Kravet fabric block light. LEFT, ABOVE All the house's bathrooms feature white powder-coated plumbing fixtures from Grohe. In the master bathroom, a Swarovski-crystal chandelier sits close to the ceiling above a spoon-shaped Corian bathtub from Blackman. RIGHT, ABOVE Throughout the house, blue often serves as an accent color. In a bathroom, a customized floral mural in the shower is pieced together with Sicis tiles. Matte stainless-steel Nessen lamps mounted onto a Corian counter reflect light into a mirror.

LEFT, ABOVE A glass-and-French-limestone staircase connects a stylish rec room to a more formal upstairs living room. RIGHT, ABOVE A sculpture in bronze of a reclining nude by Kiki Smith dips its toes into a lap pool in front of a gym enlivened by a circular canvas of Takashi Murakami's animated flowers. Barnes Coy conceived the house as a stone box within a picture frame. RIGHT A series of guestrooms—each tinted a seafoam green—wraps around a pool facing a bay. The structure's flat roof is carpeted with playfully obvious artificial grass and looks onto poolside furniture from Gervasoni, Dedon, and Patricia Urquiola. A large bird sound installation by Hiraki Sawa completes the arrangement.

The 400-square-foot living room in the 1,200-square-foot Chelsea duplex I share with Steven Wine extends onto a terrace that overlooks bustling West Twenty-third Street in Chelsea. The space contains numerous shades of white, including Venetian plaster embedded with mica dust and installed by Mile Djuric, a white cotton quilt from Nancy Koltes, and custom-knit fabric by ABYU.

TOP LEFT A staircase covered in shag carpet from Aronson's connects the entry hall to the main upper floor. It's enlivened by walls covered in aluminum leaf by Judith Eisler, a painting by Hiro Yokose, and part of my collection of taxidermy chickens. TOP RIGHT A pair of barrel-chested cabinets in the master bedroom came from an online furniture outlet; the original decorative paint was covered with several coats of white lacquer by Alpha Craft. LEFT, ABOVE In one corner, a rabbit-fur throw, two 1950s lamps, a white glass vase from End of History, and an original Casalino chair from the 1970s add texture to the space. RIGHT, ABOVE A rectangular mirror with ceramic leaves for a frame from 145 Antiques draws northern light into the master bedroom. It, in turn, reflects an original oval mirror by Giò Ponti.

TOP Former storage space is now converted into a master bathroom built for two. Duplicate sinks face each other, one room has a shower, and the other a tub. The walls to the hallway are mirrored to give this, the only room with no window, a view to the outside. LEFT, ABOVE The living room features a vintage 1970s glass-topped coffee table found on a neighborhood sidewalk; aluminum circles form its base. The collection of Jean Cocteau–style painted ceramic bowls are by Alessandro Merlin's Venetian workshop. One of them holds an 8-foot-long string of pearls from China. RIGHT, ABOVE An L-shaped sofa in the den converts into a queen-size bed; it's accompanied by a 1960s-era tea table by Richard Himmel.

White treatments reinvigorate a collection of rich wood furniture in a Shingle Style, 12,000-square-foot house in Larchmont, New York, by architect Robert Keller. In an octagonal living room, a squared-off seating configuration floats on a cream circular carpet and is anchored by a sentry-like standing lamp in each corner. White also calms the potentially busy ceiling latticework. Full draperies attach to the walls with simple boat eyehooks.

ABOVE In the octagonal master bedroom, no wall was wide enough to anchor the bed against, so a king-sized four-poster from Holly Hunt floats in the room's center instead. A Venetian lamp from Chameleon Lighting sits on a drum table by Ambience; an oval Ciao Manhattan mirror is by City Studio. RIGHT Thin black tapers extend the height of a battalion of oil-rubbed bronze candlesticks Ted Muehling designed for E. R. Butler. The collection is gathered on top of a teak cabinet in a formal dining room. The window draperies are by Hunter Douglas.

LEFT In the Scottsdale Mondrian Hotel, a Garden of Eden theme is brought into the present with a white-and-black color scheme. For the lobby, Kozan Studios fabricated six oversized lamps from fiberglass as well as an 18-foot-high representation of a baobab that's commonly referred to as the "Tree of Life." ABOVE At the entrance to a bar, my version of traditional tufted wing-back armchairs flank a curtained column and a wall of antique mirror glass. Cream silk portières frame views into several sections of the lobby.

ABOVE, LEFT A mirrored communal dining table reflects the leaflike details of a Murano glass chandelier. Reproduction Thonet chairs are arranged to seat fourteen. The restaurant represents the orchard in the Garden Of Eden. ABOVE, RIGHT An otherwise unadorned wall gains textural interest with a gridded pattern of plaster studs. Repurposed standing lamps gained a new lease on life once their shades acquired long, acrylic fringes. RIGHT An enlargement of Albrecht Durer's sixteenth-century representation of Adam and Eve adds a layer to the good-versus-evil theme—different segments of the engraving appear as a blown-up graphic throughout the hotel in bedrooms, bathrooms, and on hall walls. FAR RIGHT Plaster steer heads are Kozan Studios' reinterpretation of iconic desert imagery. Cotton lamps designed by Denis Santachiara for Studio Italia sway close to the ceiling, move sideways, and light up like sun-drenched clouds.

CLEARLY SPEAKING

I grew up on the beach. I'm still drawn to the ocean on weekends and vacations—the hypnotic sound of waves is my natural sleeping pill. Water imagery is also woven into my interiors in both obvious and subliminal ways. Up to 60 percent of our body is water, so our affinity with it in its many incarnations is primordial. Whenever I use Lucite, for example, I'm reminded of solid ice. An undulating curtain hem is reminiscent of a rippling stream. Antiqued glass has a vaporous quality. A bank of sheer fabric diffuses light like fog. And then there are all the hundreds of shades of white paint that try to capture and recreate snow's purity. On an emotional level, there's nothing more thrilling or relaxing than watching light gracefully shimmer across a pool of water—I try to bring a subtle memory of that to all my projects.

Flow, a room's directional buoyancy if you will, can sometimes seem difficult to evaluate. In simple terms, it describes a given space's most logical traffic route, but the same word is used to describe circulation patterns and the movement of water for a reason. To see if a space feels intuitive to navigate, close your eyes and imagine water slowly seeping in through each of a room's doorways. Its meandering pathway will illustrate the space's perfect flow, and you can use that mental map to help you place furnishings in a way that won't impede it.

Light shines freely through acrylics, which is why I used the material prominently in a line of furniture I designed a few years ago. As a base for a coffee or dining table, it consumes no visual mass, it dematerializes before your eyes, it allows top surfaces made of a contrasting material to float, and it has no ego about being upstaged by everything around it. It's stronger than tempered glass, it weighs less, and it's more transparent and colorless.

I'm always attracted to vintage Lucite chairs and tables I come across at auctions. If I'm customizing furniture for a particular project at the moment, I'll sometimes buy a piece just because it has the potential to inspire me—not because I intend to use it in a room. I would never duplicate a classic piece exactly. Even when the designer is unknown, which is often the case with mid-twentieth-century acrylic, I'm happy if I'm just able to capture a piece's essence.

The simplest, most low-maintenance centerpiece in the world is a lineup of unadorned, clear vases filled to the brim with water. In a variety of shapes and sizes they resemble a skyline or an architectural ice sculpture. They're a pure celebration of form. Interspersed with a few lit candles, they become kaleidoscopes of flame—and coincidentally, they double as a passive humidifier!

CHAPTER 6

PLAYING WITH ILLUSIONS

A well-designed object always stops me in my tracks and energizes me, whether it's a toothbrush, a bicycle, a shirt, or a hat. And when I lose my breath or my heart pounds the first time I encounter a space, I take my own hat off to the interior designer. If I have to analyze why I'm seduced by that space, I know it's because some illusion has been employed. Sometimes a well-designed room seems to defy analysis or logic. It just IS!

Voltaire described illusion as the first of all pleasures, and it's certainly one of the first tools a designer considers using when he or she evaluates space. It compensates for many flaws—it's a panacea. It's a noninvasive a way to disguise, emphasize, extend, exaggerate, or diminish a room's shortcomings or strengthen its assets. It can take the form of an unexpected panel of color; stripy wallpaper; waist-high horizontal paneling; high-backed furniture; or very strategic lighting. Mirrors are the ultimate space shifters, and partition walls made of sheer drapes are a close second—they offer up the same diffused view of reality as a soft-focus lens.

Translucent materials like glass and Lucite have solidity and strength, and they're two of my favorite surfaces to employ. In a room they take up no visual space, yet they alter the relative proportions and characteristics of anything nearby. A small dining space will open up miraculously when a wooden table is surrounded by a set of transparent polycarbonate chairs. It opens up even more if the wooden table is replaced with glass. And if one of the walls is mirrored, the space appears to double in size. Visual tricks only get you so far, of course, and they should necessarily be site specific. When I first became a designer, there was a trend for oversized mirrors set on the floor and leaning against a wall. It was as if the entire design industry's unanimous first response to a small room was, "How about using a gigantic mirror?" Any tactic loses its potency or becomes a cliché when it's overused.

I'm inspired by art, fashion, and cinema. I'm one of those people who watches films with the sound turned off so I can take in the production values, and in fact I first learned about manipulating perspective by studying films from the 1930s. Back then designers often created what appeared to be open, flowing room sets by building background furniture at a diminished scale. Or they placed large objects—a tall armchair or a screen—way up front to frame and heighten the apparent distance between the foreground and the horizon line. I've seen *Blade Runner* more times than I can remember; I love its brilliantly atmospheric night shots and the skillful way it completely transforms Los Angeles. Then there are the rich tapestry of visual metaphors in Jean Cocteau's *La Belle et la Bête*. And of course there's the totally inspirational *Auntie Mame*, a true crash course in avant-garde decoration with its hydraulic sofas and koi ponds.

Needless to say, it's my job to create livable environments and not movie sets. Though it's also true that we're currently living in an age where the theatricality of hotel design has infiltrated into our homes. The first time I walked into a Los Angeles hotel suite and encountered a bathtub in the center of the living room, I thought it was outrageous and fun. I took in a glamorous view of the Hollywood Hills while I bathed, and found myself questioning why we customarily shove our tubs into cramped corners. Give me a glimpse of stars over grout any day! I wouldn't plant a tub in the middle of a client's living room per se, but the experience did teach me to always explore whether it's possible to position them where they can take advantage of a pleasant view.

I take tons of pictures when I travel, but only sketching helps me to truly comprehend a space. As Henri Cartier-Bresson pointed out, "photography is an immediate reaction, drawing is a meditation." So when I sit in front of a building and put pen to paper, I'm forced to focus on the minutiae I would otherwise overlook. I zero in on things a camera judges to be inconsequential. For example, I've admired the way Borromini's churches in Rome play with space—they're famous for it—so I was taught to look intently at the way his concave and convex surfaces manipulate what we think we see. I only picked up on the subtle differences in each of the three stories on the facade of the Palazzo Farnese when I sketched it. I sketch continuously when I present a project to a client. Showing how an illusion works is much easier than trying to explain it.

PREVIOUS PAGES To lessen some of the more "masculine" traits in one of David Hertz's spectacularly detailed, modern houses in Venice, California, diaphanous floor-to-ceiling draperies soften concrete living room walls and low-slung tie-back curtains ameliorate its 18-foot height. An oval shag rug offsets the room's angularity and a 6-foot-tall, rococo-style mirror above the sofa balances high rectangular windows. LEFT A Feng Shui master prescribed a "red cure" for a portion of the dining room, so a window surround is now tinted a peony pink and draped with transparent fabric mounted on a curved track to soften the room's hard edges—the oval table's white-lacquered top also features a red underside. A mirror widens the room by triggering an infinity perspective and a high-gloss Venetian plaster ceiling animates the room.

LEFT Stylistically, a Neiman Marcus headboard upholstered in tufted silk and detailed with an antique-mirror border is akin to the bed's florid Osborne & Little fabric. Seafoam-green walls are a shade away from an adjacent bathroom's sandblasted glass. ABOVE In the master bathroom, Really Fake Digital printed and installed a mural depicting Alexandre Cabanel's *Birth of Venus*. The floor changes from wood to Bisazza tile as it approaches water fixtures; curtains diffuse sun as it streams through the skylights.

A Colonial-era house close to Princeton, New Jersey, needed its several subsequent additions to feel more stylistically cohesive. In a nineteenth-century living room with 8-foot-high ceilings, orchestrated furniture and fabric configurations make the space feel grander—an oversized Queen Anne chair wears the same silk fabric as the draperies, for example. The bone-white table is from Ambience.

TOP Dark wood paneling in the living room took on a more contemporary look after a few coats of sage green paint. A sparer approach to accessories also helped enliven the traditional space. ABOVE In an adjacent sunroom, low ceilings feel less oppressive thanks to a large, square mirror. Flanked by Nessen sconces, it absorbs a cool light from the surrounding pale-blue, slipcovered furniture. Bunches of shapely, bleached grasses qualify as a contemporary dried flower arrangement. RIGHT Penn & Fletcher's embroidered silk draperies float in a doorway between the sunroom and living room. A John Saladino sofa sits on a carpet Mark Nelson designed for Patterson, Flynn & Martin.

ABOVE In a formerly dark dining room in the older part of the house, Christophe Pourny resurfaced the walls in a lavender purple—the client's favorite color—and artist Judith Eisler painted a faux-mirror finish onto the ceiling. Neoclassical Baker chairs wear organza "shoulder wraps" while a trio of small glass-cluster chandeliers span the table's length. RIGHT A breakfast room in the modern part of the Princeton house overlooks an immense, rambling English garden. Its ceiling pitches to 20 feet, so tented draperies enhance its natural theatrical flair. The oak table is from Zona and the metal chairs are from ABC Carpet & Home.

The design challenge with Villa Roxie, the Mediterranean-style mansion Lenny Kravitz named after his late mother, actress Roxie Roker, was how to stylistically integrate its many rooms. An intimate, limited palette of silvery whites was employed throughout the house, particularly in this meditation room where spray-painted teak chairs anchor a Mongolian lamb fur rug and leather fringes from low-hung ceiling fixtures cascade down onto stainless-steel side tables.

ABOVE Oversized terra-cotta planters filled with shaggy grasses line an entrance to the villa's game room. Sunbrella drapes and filigreed Moroccan lanterns set the scene for a set of Verner Panton's cantilevered stacking chairs in a loggia. RIGHT, BELOW A pool table from Blatt Billiards was lacquered in white to give it a more tropical feel. Part of Kravitz's vast African mask collection is mounted as a high frieze along the length of a khaki wall. The coffers of the teak ceiling dictated the proportions of the oversized, dice-like acrylic light fixtures. FAR RIGHT This outdoor dining area on the ground floor of a guest wing next to a canal could be situated in a Venetian palazzo. Oversized glass orbs from Lunatika hang from an ornately carved wood ceiling above a pedestal table from Cobweb.

OVERLEAF A silver-and-gold-leafed throne chair upholstered in white rabbit reportedly belonged to Cardinal Spellman. It now sits at a desk that cantilevers out from the back of a headboard in the master suite. A silver-sequined bedspread ties in visually with a silver chain mail curtain that loops around the bed to form a circular enclosure within a square room.

PREVIOUS PAGES On Manhattan's Upper East Side an awkwardly configured 1,100-square-foot penthouse was given an easier flow between rooms and a feeling of spaciousness thanks in part to a room-wide sofa that de-emphasizes the non-symmetrically beamed ceiling. Walls painted with Benjamin Moore's Florida Aqua pick up on the broadloom carpet David Hockney designed for Relative Space. Hockney's own habit of wearing mismatched socks inspired the different seat colors on the Eero Saarinen Tulip chairs. LEFT A shelf unit made from four colors of Edgeglow Acrylic by Just Plastics dematerializes the apartment's entrance hall. Since it sits against a mirror and its geometrically plumb set of drawers, cubby holes, and shelves graduate in size, it creates an optical illusion that makes it impossible to estimate the tiny space's actual dimensions. ABOVE Four Tulip chairs tuck under a long, narrow table in one corner of a tiny dining room where two peach-glazed, mirrored walls abut; their double reflections amplify the setting's width and depth. A red La Murrina chandelier in the living room even seems to become part of the space.

PREVIOUS PAGES In Soho, a living room's grand-salon personality emerged once a wall of backlit curtains replaced a formal entrance and once we shortened the ceiling by two feet. Now guests who enter from a lower level don't register a windowless space—instead, they're wooed by its perfect proportions. A wall of mirrors and three separate seating areas are united by a circular table at the center. LEFT Thanks to a stylized, symmetrical layout and three separate sitting areas, a regular Upper East Side TV room becomes a sophisticated boudoir. Painted and upholstered in gold, several shades of white, and subtle lime green—the client's favorite color—a 1940s sofa and armchairs by Jean Royère along with fake fur, long tassels, Mongolian lamb lap rugs, feather lampshades, and pearl-accessorized chairs give the space a vaguely retro feel.

ABOVE A relatively small dining room situated between a kitchen and a long hallway escapes the city's noise and bustle. The Buddha oil painting is from the client's collection, a wooden Thai gate was hung as art, and the glass chandelier came from Marvin Alexander.

ABOVE In a dining room, elaborate Egyptian chairs team up with a pair of simpler, lined-corduroy upholstered benches around a customized Ambience table. A silk carpet below adds subtle color. RIGHT We converted this apartment's existing master suite into a sizable den and tented a smaller foyer space with sixty yards of powder-blue voile to create an alternative bedroom. Blue-and-white glass Chameleon lamps now occupy side tables in the dreamlike setting.

In a high-rise building located on Manhattan's West Side Highway, a silvery-gray interior spray-painted by Gotham Painting glows every evening as the setting sun reflects off the Hudson River. The metallic monochrome visually enlarges the space's height and width. A wide array of furnishings including a 1930s sofa, an oval Biedermeier table, an Eero Saarinen 1948 Womb chair, and a high-powered telescope defy any particular stylistic categorization.

LEFT Cut-away sides on smoked acrylic chairs from the 1970s mimic the curved arms of a candelabrum Borek Sipek designed in the late 1980s. Several rows of mirrored paillettes attached to the ceiling with clear fishing wire scatter light like deconstructed disco balls.

ABOVE A cantilevered piece of clear acrylic serves as a bar/breakfast table and demarcates the line between the kitchen and living rooms in the small space. Metal stools continue the silver theme.

WARRIOR-PROPHET

PREVIOUS PAGES Simply because it had two doors, this a room in a Chelsea, Manhattan, apartment felt like a thoroughfare. The clients wanted it to function as a self-contained dining room where guests felt coddled and enveloped instead, so a soothing light butterscotch color now bathes the walls—the wood floors and upholstery on the Ludwig Mies van der Rohe chairs match to within a couple of shades. The acrylic table base recedes visually and a tubular glass chandelier designed by ABYU Lighting casts an intimate light. LEFT In the master bedroom, a mirrored wall appropriates the views and air space of an outdoor terrace. In a 4-foot-wide passage behind the bed, a desk recesses into a wall of storage. A paneled, leather-upholstered headboard houses a series of square lights. ABOVE This bathroom functions as a steam room with bench capacity for eight people. Soft lighting, Sorrell cabinets and infinity mirrors on one large, continuous wall prevent it from seeming too institutional.

CURTAIN CALLS

Floor-to-ceiling curtains are architectural elements. They're also a practical and sometimes ethereal way to apportion space. I often use them to unite a row of windows, camouflage a wall of appliances, compartmentalize a bed, help contour a boxy vestibule, or monumentalize a headboard. When they ribbon freely through a space, they suggest a unique circulation pattern.

Curtains are stylistically compatible with every type of space when hung from recessed ceiling tracks, whether constructed from translucent or opaque fabrics. I've used them to bring human scale to a gymnasium-sized loft and to convert a remote utility closet into an extroverted backstage. They do have to be used in broad strokes. For example, to cordon off a 3-foot-wide entry to a hallway, I widen the curtain until it touches the farthest perimeters of the hallway's neighboring walls. It creates architectural grandeur; installing curtains of the hall's exact width would have made the gesture feel skimpy.

I apply the same principle to windows. I never corral them with heavy treatments, never straitjacket them with ruffles, swags, or complicated passementerie. Think of a window as a vehicle for light. If you approach it as one component of a blank wall's face, then there's no reason to isolate it or gussy it up as the main focal point. Compare an overdressed window to an overly wrought, scene-stealing frame around a minimalist painting. They're both superfluous. Multiple layers of elaborately tailored fabrics are popular traditional drapery treatments, but they're overkill in a modern interior. Tie back a simple, gauzelike curtain with a traditional tassle instead to complement classical architectural detailing. Weighty curtains may keep out glare, but they stifle luminescence in the bargain.

Skip linings if you don't want to muffle a fabric's intrinsic beauty, but always be generous with yardage. Volume feels exuberant. Make curtains 60 percent wider than the window. Voile and chiffon have a luscious weightlessness if you're looking for transparency; consider worsted wools for opaques. Don't be afraid to look into synthetics for high-traffic areas; we install vinyl curtains in hotels and apartment lobbies where durability and cleaning are the most important concerns—the latest textiles feel as luxe as cashmere, and their concentrated weave rarely needs a hem. Movement is a large part of a curtain's appeal, so let it puddle slightly onto the floor to avoid having it look too rigid.

I often expose hardware, and even when I embed hospital tracks into sheetrock I leave the hooks visible. I think of it in the same way as deconstructed fashion. Sometimes we even equip a Roman shade with extra, nonfunctional pulleys to give it a hint of an industrial aesthetic, and in my book that counts as ornamentation!

CHAPTER 7

COLORFUL CHARACTERS

I wear black quite often, but I rarely use it in my interiors—not even on the subtlest piece of trim. As a child growing up in the Caribbean, graphite skies portended hurricanes that would invariably bring with them trails of destruction and sadness. I've never been able to completely rid myself of that unhappy association. In fact, it's hard for me to tolerate any dark color if it's dull or tends toward gloomy. I prefer to stay in the realm of bright and optimistic hues. I also stay away from in-between shades that tend to change dramatically with the light, like periwinkle or any reds that veer pink, because I don't feel like I can ever truly control the way they will appear. Deep reds, however, flatter food and people so they're great candidates for institutional work, although I have to keep in mind that if a woman applied makeup in a red bathroom she might walk out looking like a clown! *Bruma*, the Spanish word for haze that doesn't have a great English counterpart in the color realm, is an all-time favorite. I love the way it resembles the blue-green of sea water as it's filtered through the foaming crest of a wave.

To get back to my point: color preference is highly individual and is heavily based on our past experiences. Jorge Luis Borges expressed this notion in a beautifully poetic way: "I saw a sunset in Querétaro that seemed to reflect the color of a rose in Bengal." We all have similar thoughts—often intensely emotional—about why we like blue or why we avoid gray or pink. I had an unforgettable experience while I was still working with John Saladino. We'd selected a beautiful magenta palette for a lobby but when we presented it to the architect, I. M. Pei, he rejected it straightaway. He said it reminded him of a brothel. To John and I, the color was distinctly papal. Our responses couldn't have been more different! (The lobby, predictably, ended up a noncommittal beige.) Color is the most versatile tool in a designer's kit and the quickest, least expensive, least intrusive way to totally reinvent a space, but I tread very carefully when I propose bold hues to clients.

Because of all of its associative properties—good and bad—color can add more spice to a space than any individual object. It can be tricky to select a color until you actually see it on the wall, however, because it visually bleeds onto its neighbors and changes according to its background. One of my radical maneuvers is to select one strong color and apply it to an entire room. It instantly disguises generic architecture, brings pizzazz into a basement space, or satisfies a client who's in need of a megadose of theatricality. When a monochrome—be it pink, puce, or pomegranate—is splashed across a room's walls and ceiling and there's no other color in close proximity, it mysteriously takes on the characteristics of a neutral. All color is no color! People with real flair have gamblers' hearts, and I'm fortunate to have adventurous clients who are brave enough to take on cobalt blue, canary yellow, and scarlet rooms. Committing to an abundance of one color makes an incredibly bold statement so it's not for the fainthearted.

To be clear, when I refer to painting a room all in one color I mean several different shades of the same hue. I would never paint a room in just one value—it would only feel surreal and agitating. Graduated shades, however, are optically peaceful. When hue intensities have subtle variations, shapes and surface planes flatten and appear to be contiguous. When values contrast more sharply they produce a discernible depth of field as objects and planes separate from each another visually. A monochrome also affects how we register scale. Closely related values and hues seem to increase the size of a small room while marked contrasts of color, hue, intensity, and value make a large room seem smaller.

Calibrate a room's color according to the amount of incoming natural light. If it's in abundance, opt for paleness. When it's scarce, indulge your eye with darker shades. Rather than trying to follow conflicting rules you read in shelter magazines, let intuition guide your decisions. Camp out in a space until you've ascertained its mood—or take a more random approach and let the room suggest the final color to you. Settle on a color that complements an exterior view if it's remarkable. When all else fails: go with a color purely because it's your favorite.

PREVIOUS PAGES For a master bedroom in a suburban New York house, fabrics in a soothing shade of periwinkle are paired with paint color in the same hue but at a 50 percent less-intense saturation. A wood tansu chest, a white lamp, and a gold mirror frame provide the only contrasting colors. ABOVE In the house's dining room, a team of four benches upholstered in Almost Leather vinyl and four baronial velvet-covered chairs prevent a 14-foot-long dining table from feeling corporate. A translucent lace runner diminishes its prominence even more while colored cotton curtains provide privacy. To complete the monochromatic effect, the walls are painted Benjamin Moore's Million Dollar Red. RIGHT A sunflower-yellow living room complements greenery outside the windows. The chair, sofa, and Roman shades are all the same Covington fabric. The presence of a wooden chair frame and sisal carpet ground the yellow, while a white lamp and table make it appear crisp.

LEFT Color lends the rooms in a Central Park apartment a multitude of personalities. The living room feels serene thanks to extremely white walls and two focally placed chaises that wear diaphanous silk slipcovers. Solid wood and metal furniture lend masculinity. OVERLEAF, LEFT In a north-facing bedroom, a vintage Fortuny bedspread and a sensually lined headboard upholstered in Gretchen Bellinger velvet lend glamour to a bed that floats, stagelike, in the center of the room. Celadon-colored walls and carpeting and a handful of other green shades—hunter, fern, jade, forest, and asparagus—flatter a small collection of Middle Eastern furniture. OVERLEAF, RIGHT Apart from a rustic pine cabinet, a Biedermeier side chair wearing a negligée-like silk slipcover, and a black-and-white photograph of Marilyn Monroe, every element in this small library is midnight blue—including glazed walls, taffeta-and-voile shades, and a chaise tufted with Gretchen Bellinger Scala mohair.

PREVIOUS PAGES In a 3,000-square-foot Park Avenue apartment, crinkly blue taffeta lavishly skirts a round table that is clearly the belle of a large living room. The fabric provides a central jolt of color in a fairly conservative, neutral layout. It's also highly functional: with the aid of concealed wire pulleys it lifts, like a theatrical curtain whenever the client's son wants to use the room's uncarpeted floor as a tricycle racetrack. LEFT Blue is often associated with depth, harmony, and stability. In this apartment's entry hall it envelops a folding screen, a Chinese table, and a Queen Anne chair to give continuity to an enclosed space. A peacock-feather shade by ABYU Lighting breathes new life into a crystal baluster lamp base. ABOVE A hall door opens onto the living room, where a mahogany-stained oak floor appears as a large color plane; the blue-to-brown juxtaposition subconsciously creates an earth/sky analogy.

LEFT A mustard-and-claret dining room feels perpetually autumnal and was inspired by the client's collection of 1970s glass vases. Chairs are either lacquered in red or wear a sari-like silk slipcover. ABOVE This apartment was a rental, so the clients were leery of removing a toile wallpaper in the den. Its busyness subsided and its intensity lessened once we hung a "tapestry" of channel-quilted Larsen fabric above a velvet sofa against one wall. Flanking it are a collection of black-and-white photographs and a pair of Ingo Maurer's iconic Lampampes. OVERLEAF Blue allowed us to harmonize a client's diverse furniture inventory in a Tribeca guestroom. Apart from a shiny, round, white acrylic tabletop and the silver dome of Achille Castiglioni's iconic Arco lamp, all the surfaces are matte.

LEFT Intense color reads as a neutral yet dramatizes a nondescript hallway in this apartment. Closet doors are now hidden behind double-width taffeta curtains opposite a square mirror that reflects two walls painted in Benjamin Moore's Cottage Red. ABOVE Neighboring buildings inspired the living room's yellow-peach palette. A daybed with custom chenille upholstery by Jeffrey Aronoff is the sole piece of furniture that sits parallel to the architecture—chairs, chaises, tables, and sofas with windowsill-or-lower profiles and curvy silhouettes were selected to give the room a perception of additional height and movement.

LEFT Cuban-tiled floors original to this 1930s Miami stucco house inspired the choice of the mango color in a ballroom-sized living room with 15-foot-high ceilings. The white denim upholstery and white fabric wainscoting prevent the intense yellow from reflecting unattractively onto seated guests' faces. ABOVE A faux-marble fireplace surround with a screen made from bicycle reflectors was inspired by a Paco Rabanne mesh; it flickers at night by candlelight. The exposed-aluminum wainscoting track traverses windows and walls so it reads like jewelry for the room. Its mechanical simplicity allows for curtains to be easily removed and washed.

ABOVE The nearby ocean and the Greek island of Santorini inspired the blue-and-white color scheme of this guest bedroom. A white matelassé coverlet provides textural contrast to the smooth, Covington fabric–covered toss pillows. RIGHT Upstairs, all the rooms radiate outward from a marigold-yellow landing. A second guest bedroom draws its color scheme from a bed of Birds of Paradise flowers that surround the house. Taken out of its normal context, a simple wood-handled painter's lamp from a local hardware store provides a note of industrial glamour.

PREVIOUS PAGES A Medici portrait inspired the décor's overall color and patterning scheme for this Park Avenue apartment. A rococo gilt mirror was the first purchase a client and I made for the space; it now presides over the living room like a heraldic shield and floats against heavily pleated gold taffeta drapes. The Gustavian sofa wears a Cowtan & Tout brocade, and the oversized ottoman with floor-length fringing features quilted Gretchen Bellinger fabric. ABOVE All the mocha-colored upholstery in this library is of a single source: Gretchen Bellinger's Limousine cloth. Artist Judith Eisler glazed the ceiling and Christophe Pourny finished the room's oak cabinetry to give it an aged, smoky feeling. RIGHT In the dining room rich, formal elements shine in a contemporary context. Pale sage-green walls and uncarpeted parquet allow a freestanding, embossed leather screen in a document brocade from Yale Burge to take prominence—it also disguises a stored, 7-foot-diameter tabletop the client uses whenever seating for twelve is required. For more intimate meals, damask-upholstered chairs provide a small pedestal table with comfortable seating.

COVER STORIES

Textiles infuse a home with its sensuality and personality. In our office, swatches from all the top fabric houses sit in towering stacks of see-through boxes catalogued by color. Generally my search for the perfect curtain fabric begins by considering its purpose. Do I need it to drape, fold, puddle, flow, shimmer, flutter, or even just stand up to prolonged wear? As far as upholstery fabric is concerned, the right combination of texture, color, and pattern allow any piece of furniture to cop an attitude and flaunt its curves and angles. With the right covering, even the most mainstream silhouette acquires some swagger.

There was a time when chintzes and moirés equaled fancy, formal good taste. Nowadays the design pedigrees of different styles are totally mixed and people take unconventional ideas in stride. On the other hand, the use of fur still sends out a controversial message. I only source the skins of animals I eat, so I'm comfortable installing sheepskin or cowhide rugs. I wouldn't dream of working with anything rare, exotic, or extinct. A few years ago a client took her grandmother's leopard-skin coat out of mothballs and asked us to turn it into a handful of sofa pillows. I love recycling so I thought it was a great idea. Boy, did we receive a slew of irate letters from readers once the project appeared in a magazine. Since then, I've grown to love fake fur.

I never restrict myself to the function a fabric's label suggests. That is, I use upholstery-weight textiles for curtains and vice versa. If it suits my visual purpose, I'll line a wall or a headboard with a fashion fabric because I'm confident that Kenny Flam, who I've worked with for decades, will intuitively know how to fortify it. Fashion is a constant source of inspiration, so I may have a Balenciaga ball gown in mind when I ask Kenny to cut some damask for a circular tablecloth on the bias. Or maybe the oversized topstitching on a Lanvin jacket or the box pleats of a Rei Kawakubo tunic affect how I ask him to finish a set of linen draperies. If I'm covering a sofa in a den where kids and pets have free rein, of course I'll use a known entity—something heavy-duty and washable. But I'll take liberties with a hall chair if it's only used as a perch once in a while. Maybe I'll slipcover it with a reinforced organza or an embroidered voile? With added backing, even stretchy terry cloth and jersey knits function well on an occasional seat.

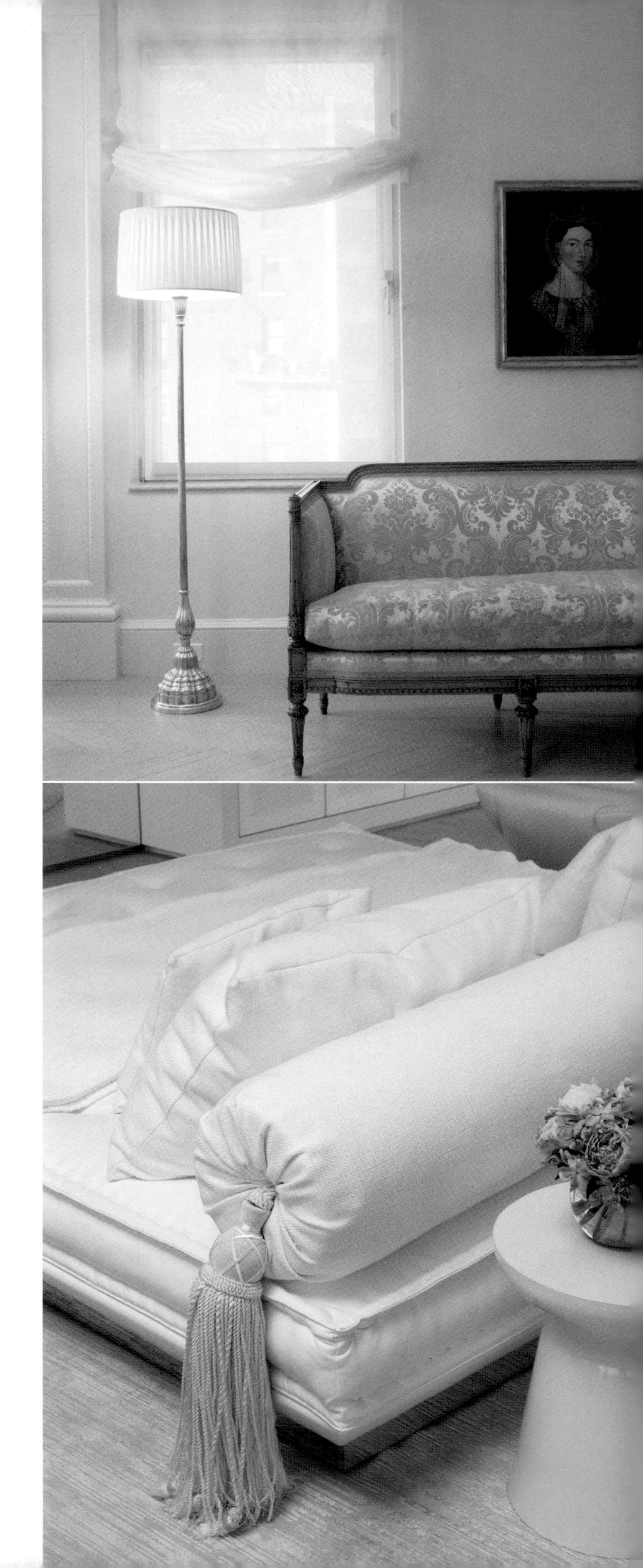

ACKNOWLEDGMENTS

Fifteen years of Linda O'Keeffe's professional encouragement led me to embark on this monograph. Heartfelt thanks to her for the elegant creative direction and for writing words that echo my voice so accurately.

I am indebted to Elizabeth Sverbeyeff Byron, the first architecture editor to discover my work. Her cover story in 1994 and respected endorsement gave my projects an international recognition. Veteran design editors Sarah Medford and Newell Turner also championed my work early on, as did Dara Caponigro. I'm grateful for the industry support I received from tastemakers Donna Warner, Mayer Rus, Julie Iovine, Wendy Goodman, Mike Strohl, Jacqueline Goewey, Doretta Sperduto, Carolyn Solis, Judith Gura, Elana Frankel, Rima Suqi, Cindy Allen, Jason Kontos, Doris Chevron, Dominick Bradbury, Sarah Lynch, Mark Luscombe-Whyte, Suzanne Slesin, Lisa Newsom, Samantha Nestor, and Pilar Viladas.

Thanks also to feature writers Jen Renzi, Michael Lassell, Judith Nasatir, Alejandro Saralegui, Jorge S. Arango, David Keeps, Michele Keith, Paula Rice Jackson, Kira Wilson Gould, Claudia Steinberg, Robert E. Bryan, Susan Kleinman, Arlene Hirst, Michael Cunningham, Christine Pittel, Dylan Landis, Elizabeth Hunter, Lisa Skolnik and Fred Bernstein for explaining my work so eloquently.

Peter Margonelli's images first captured the essence of my designs so beautifully. My dear friend Antoine Bootz also continues the photographic documentation process in his uniquely artful way. Special thanks to Simona Aru and Lucca Guarneri, Quentin Bacon, Pieter Estersohn, Michael Grimm, Joshua McHugh, Michael Luppino, Peter Murdock, Mark Seliger, Tom Sibley, Irvin Serrano, Michael Mundy, Marc Scrivo, Ellen Silverman, and Barbel Miebach, whose photographs all grace the pages of this volume.

Thank you to The Monacelli Press for believing in my aesthetic, particularly to Stacee Gravelle Lawrence for her endless patience and insightful guidance, and to Michael Vagnetti. Thanks are also due to Karen Hsu for her inspired layouts.

I extend my gratitude to all my clients, especially Deborah and David McCourt and Nancy and Steve Fabrikant, my first clients, for their unwavering faith. Thanks also to all the clients who entrusted me to design multiple homes for them over many years—Gail & Al Engelberg, Judy and W. Brian Little, Ben Jacobson, Dian Woodner, Mark Perlbinder, Steve Brown and Steve Saide, Sandra Eu, Laurence Isaacson, Joe De Matteo, Sean Cassidy and Gerry Logue, Laura Esquivel, Kathy Jaharis, Lenny Kravitz, Warrie & Jim Price, Sean Combs, Melani and Randy Nardone, Francesco Piovanetti, Tina & Simon Oxenham, and Debbie & Mitch Rechler.

I'm also grateful to clients who allowed me to venture into the worlds of retail and hospitality—W Hotels, Morgans Hotel Group, Kohler Company, Cartier, Diptyque, Barney's, Tracie Martyn, Cape Advisors, Alchemy Properties, and Ivanka Trump.

Special thanks for the encouragement and support of my friends David Landis, David Plante, Robert Farrell, Ed and Lisa Baquero, Virginia Cobb, Nisi Berryman, David Vigliano, Patricia Field, Andrea Schwan, and Rhett Butler, whose creative risk-taking and business acumen are on a par with none other.

I've had the great pleasure to collaborate with many fine artists and extend my appreciation to Judy Eisler, Mile Djuric, Michael Letzig, Christophe Pourny, Marcia Lippman, Heller Gallery, Beth Lipman, Thomas Thompson, and Tim McAuley as well as Eileen and Kenny Flam, whose upholstery and draperies display the craftsmanship of a Savile Row tailor. Special mention is due to artist, master interior designer, and mentor John Saladino, who launched me on this journey.

A cohesive team stands behind the scenes of every one of my projects and I have great respect for contractors Nick Zaharakis, Mary and John Rusk, Richard Fiore, Silverlining Interiors, Inc., architect Brad Zizmor from a +i—for whom no detail is too small—and for vendors Nessen, Just Plastics, Plexicraft, Mark Nelson, Aronson's, Jeffrey Aronoff, Frank Carfaro, Mazanares Furniture Corp, Gretchen Bellinger, Angela Brown, and ABYU Lighting, whose commitment to excellence always produces amazing results. Thanks also to licensing agent Greg Vargo.

Architect Brian E. Boyle deserves a special mention. May our collaboration and friendship endure for at least another two decades.

Fond thanks to my first studio employees Magali Bermudez and C. Michael Diaz; to my former team Paul Latham, Andy Suvalski, Marla Pasareno, Sarah Magness, Marisa Gomez, and Dina Feiglin, who now head their own firms; and my current team Dragan Dejkanovic, Maxime Leroy-Tullie, Scott Kochlefl, Kevin Hoffmann, Kyle O'Connor, Wayne Woodward, and Ann Das, who energize me daily with their talents.

Thanks to my ever-supportive and loving family. Endless thanks to my husband, artist Steven Jeffrey Wine, who is unconditionally there for me on a daily basis.